grade **3**

The MAILBOX® LANGUAGE ARTS INDEPENDENT PRACTICE SUPER BOOK SALE!

W9-CHT-056

 **144** EASY-TO-USE IDEAS FOR SKILL REINFORCEMENT

 Reading comprehension

 Language conventions

 Literary response

 Reference skills

 Vocabulary

 Word skills

 Writing

 AND LOTS MORE!

ENOUGH FOR

4 activities for every week

OF THE SCHOOL YEAR!

Managing Editor: Jennifer Bragg

Editorial Team: Becky S. Andrews, Debbie Ashworth, Diane Badden, Bonnie Baumgras, Kimberley Bruck, Karen A. Brudnak, Kitty Campbell, Jennifer Cripe, Chris Curry, Lynette Dickerson, Juli Engel, Jean Erickson, Ann Fisher, Theresa Lewis Goode, Tazmen Hansen, Marsha Heim, Lori Z. Henry, Jennifer L. Kohnke, Debra Liverman, Dorothy C. McKinney, Thad H. McLaurin, Jennifer Mross, Sharon Murphy, Jennifer Nunn, Mark Rainey, Hope Rodgers, Eliseo De Jesus Santos II, Rebecca Saunders, Renee Silliman, Crissie Stephens, Donna K. Teal, Joshua Thomas, Zane Williard

www.themailbox.com

©2008 The Mailbox® Books
All rights reserved.
ISBN10 #1-56234-841-8 • ISBN13 #978-156234-841-0

Manufactured in the United States
10 9 8 7 6 5 4 3 2 1

Table of Contents

Super Simple Independent Practice: Language Arts • ©The Mailbox® Books • TEC61150

To use the table of contents as a checklist, make a copy of pages 2 and 3. Staple or clip each copy on top of its original page. Each time you use an activity, check its box. Start each school year with fresh copies of the pages.

Skills Index
on pages 111-112.

Covered!

High-frequency words

Materials:
student copies of the gameboard on page 76
copy of the word cards on page 76, cut apart
6 index cards, each labeled with a different number
    from 1 through 6
die

A student labels each section of the gameboard with a different word from the cards. She shuffles the cards, then places four cards facedown on each numbered index card. Next, the student rolls a die, reads the cards from the corresponding pile, and places the cards on the matching gameboard squares. Play continues until one vertical or horizontal row is filled.

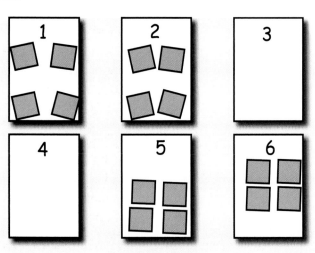

COVERED!					
about	because	their	friend	our	special
every	shown	could	people	there	just
used	guess	said	during	receive	until
read	often	idea	know	laugh	thought

Train of Events

Story events

Materials:
index cards (five per student)
construction paper
tape
crayons
scissors

After reading a story, a student writes the book's title and author on a card. Then the student writes sentences and draws pictures about the story's main events on the remaining cards. He decorates the cards with construction paper cutouts so that they resemble a train. Then he tapes the cards together.

Big Anthony and the Magic Ring
by Tomie dePaola

First Strega Nona tells Big Anthony to go to the village dance to perk himself up.

Next Big Anthony watches Strega Nona magically change into a beautiful lady.

Then Big Anthony uses Strega Nona's ring and changes into a handsome man, but when he tries to take off the ring it is stuck.

Finally, Strega Nona helps Big Anthony remove the ring with olive oil.

It's a Date!

Commas

Materials:
4 sets of color-coded, labeled index cards: days, months, numbers 1–31, years
2 small cards, each labeled with a comma
paper

The student puts one card from each set in order to make a date. She inserts the comma cards between the appropriate words and numbers and then copies the date on her paper. She creates several more dates in the same manner.

| Monday | , | September | 22 | , | 2008 |

Mara

Monday, September 22, 2008

Ready for Action

Verbs

Materials:
backpack containing props that suggest action
paper

Possible props include a *jump rope, ball, spoon, ruler,* and *cup.*

A child selects a prop from the backpack and brainstorms actions associated with it. He uses an action word and names the prop in a sentence. Then he underlines the verb and illustrates his sentence. He repeats the process on the back with another prop.

Nicole <u>bounces</u> a ball at recess.

Thesaurus Practice

Synonyms

Materials:
cards labeled with words that have synonyms
paper
thesaurus
die

> Possible words include *say, happy, sad, run, nice, funny, look, fast, slow, mad, get, make, pretty, good,* and *bad.*

A child writes a word from a card on her paper and rolls the die. She uses the number rolled as the number of synonyms to list on her paper. After she writes her list, the student refers to the thesaurus to confirm her work. Then she chooses another card and repeats the process on the back of her paper.

Flip Over Writing!

Contractions

Materials:
cards labeled with contractions
sticky notes
sentence strips
stapler

A student reads the contraction on a card and writes it on a sticky note. Then he writes on a sentence strip a sentence that uses the contraction on the sticky note. He lifts the sticky note and writes the word or words that make the contraction on the back. Then the student staples the note to the strip.

Macaroni in the Middle

Commas

Materials:
sentence strips labeled with capital cities (in red)
    and states (in blue)
dry macaroni
paper

A student reads the city and state listed on a sentence strip and places a macaroni comma between the two names. She copies each city and state pair on her paper, being sure to add the comma in the appropriate place.

Harrisburg, Pennsylvania

Denver, Colorado

Tallahassee, Florida

Name That Page

Table of contents

Materials:
student copies of page 77
2 different textbooks

A student uses the table of contents in each textbook to complete the activity.

Name: Bailey — Table of contents

Name That Page
Use two different textbooks to complete the charts.

Title of book: World of Science	Title of book: Understanding Our World
How many chapters are there? 15	How many chapters are there?
On what page does chapter 4 begin? 58	On what page does chapter 4 begin?
In which chapter would you find page 22? chapter 2	In which chapter would you find page 22?
Does the book have a glossary? yes If so, write the glossary's first word. absorption	Does the book have a glossary? If so, write the glossary's first word.
On what page does the index begin? page 215	On what page does the index begin?
Which chapter is the longest? chapter 11	Which chapter is the longest?
Which chapter is the shortest? chapter 9	Which chapter is the shortest?
Which chapter title interests you the most? "From a Seed to a Flower"	Which chapter title interests you the most?

Raindrop Race

Long vowels

Materials:
cloud and raindrop templates (patterns on page 78)
1" x 18" strips of white paper (two per child)
construction paper: white, blue
scissors
glue

A child traces and cuts two clouds from white construction paper; then he glues a paper strip at the bottom of each cloud as shown. Next, he labels one cloud "rain" and the other "day." Then the student traces and cuts several raindrops from blue construction paper. He programs each raindrop with a different word that matches the vowel patterns. Then he glues the raindrops on the corresponding strips.

Towering Book Report

Story elements

Materials:
12" x 18" light-colored construction paper (one sheet per child)
2" x 5" paper rectangles (one per child)
straws (one per child)
glue
tape
crayons

After reading a story, a student folds a sheet of construction paper to make four columns and then unfolds the paper. She labels each of the first three columns with a different story element, as shown, and draws pictures that represent each one. She refolds the paper and glues the last fold underneath the first to create a three-sided tower. Next, the student writes the book's title and author on a paper rectangle and tapes a straw on the back to make a flag. The student tapes the flag behind one of the tower's folds.

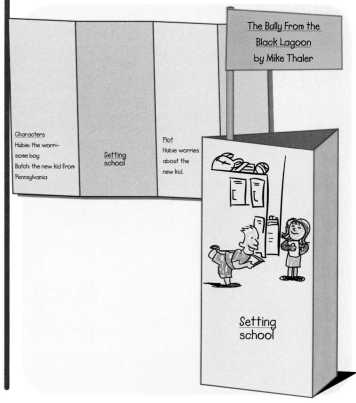

Places to Go

Capitalization

Materials:
student copies of the recording sheet on page 78
student atlas or world map

A student uses the atlas or map to locate geographic names for each letter of the alphabet and writes each name on the recording sheet.

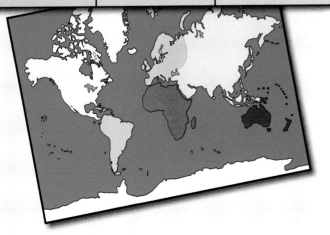

Name	Connor		
Capitalize the World			
A Australia	B Brazil	C China
D Denmark	E	F
G	H	I
J	K	L
M	N	O
P	Q	R
S	T	U
V	W	X
Y	Z	

Perfect Statements

Topic sentence

Materials:
magazines
paper
scissors
glue

A child cuts out an interesting magazine picture and glues it on her paper. Next, she writes a topic sentence about the picture and underlines it. Then she writes supporting detail sentences.

The little girl is a good student.
She gets all her work right.
The girl brings home her schoolwork.
Her family hangs the papers on the refrigerator.

Mikayla

Left Foot, Right Foot

Antonyms

Materials:
student copies of page 79

A student uses the recording sheet to list as many antonym pairs as he can name.

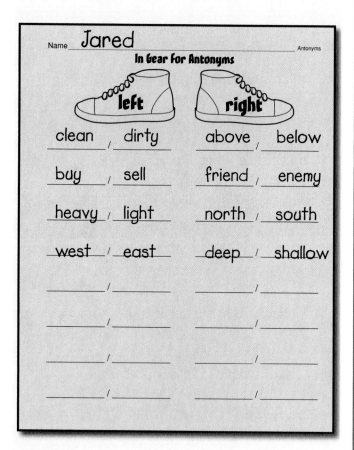

Uncovering Words

Prefixes

Materials:
list of base words
12" x 18" drawing paper (one per child)
dictionary
scissors

> Possible base words include *cover, cut, equal, fasten, happy, healthy, lock, lucky, pack, paid, plug, stable, tangle, tidy, tie, wise, wrap,* and *zip.*

A child folds and cuts a sheet of drawing paper to make a flip booklet as shown. Using the word list, she copies, defines, and illustrates a different base word on each flap. The student lifts each flap and writes the prefix *un-* with the corresponding base word. She defines and illustrates the resulting words.

Punctuating Practice

Periods

Materials:
magnetic surface
round magnets (periods)
sentence strips labeled with abbreviated titles
    and initials without periods
paper

A student places a sentence strip on a magnetic surface and then uses magnets to punctuate the initials or title. She copies the punctuated name on her paper and continues in this manner until all the strips are completed.

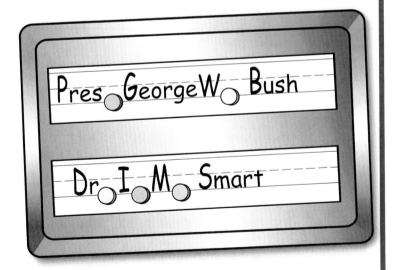

Picture This!

Prewriting

Materials:
2 sets of craft sticks labeled with common characters
    (in red) and settings (in blue)
12" x 16" construction paper (one sheet per child)
paper
stapler

A student chooses at least one craft stick from each set and brainstorms ideas for a wordless picture book. He illustrates his story and then staples the illustrated pages between a folded sheet of construction paper to make a book cover. Then, at another time, the student uses his illustrations to guide his writing.

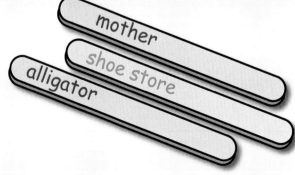

Red-Letter Words

Long vowels

Materials:
student copies of the word cards on page 80
red marker
paper
scissors
glue

A student uses a red marker to trace the vowel pairs on each word card. She cuts the cards apart and then folds a sheet of paper in half and unfolds it. The student labels each column with a vowel pair and sorts the cards according to the vowel pattern. Then she glues each card in the corresponding column.

RSVP ASAP

Abbreviations

Materials:
list of abbreviations
large index cards (one per child)

A student draws a picture of a special event on one side of an index card. Then he writes an invitation to the event on the other side, using as many abbreviations as possible.

Brief Book Reviews

Story elements

Materials:
large seasonal template
construction paper (one sheet per child)
scissors

After a student reads a book, she traces the template on her paper and cuts it out. Then she writes on the cutout the book's title, author, characters, and setting, as well as a three-to-five sentence summary of the story's events.

Title: The Vanishing Pumpkin
Author: Tony Johnston
Characters: 700-year-old woman and an 800-year-old man
Setting: around the house, along a country road
Summary: The sun reminds the old woman of pumpkins. She wants to make a pie but can't find her pumpkin. So the old man and woman go out looking for it. They meet many strange creatures along the way, including a wizard. He has the pumpkin.

Carolyn

Sentence or Not?

Complete and incomplete sentences

Materials:
copy of the sentence cards on page 80, cut apart
paper
crayons

A student reads each sentence card and then sorts it into one of two sets: complete or incomplete. He puts the incomplete sentences aside and puts the complete sentences in order to make a paragraph. Then he copies the paragraph on a sheet of paper and draws a picture.

Bob's new soccer ball is missing.

First, he searched in his room.

Next, he looked in the hall closet.

Finally, he went down to the basement.

That is where he found his new soccer ball.

Finally, he to the basement.

That where found new soccer ball.

Jake

Bob's new soccer ball is missing. First, he searched in his room. Next, he looked in the hall closet. Finally, he went down to the basement. That is where he found his new soccer ball.

Good, Better, and Best

Comparatives and superlatives

Materials:
construction paper (one sheet per child)
list of adjectives
scissors
stapler

Possible adjectives include *bright, clean, dark, dirty, fast, happy, loud, old, quiet, sad, short, slow, tall, warm, wet,* and *young.*

A student cuts her paper in half lengthwise. She layers the two sheets so the edges are about an inch apart. Then she folds and staples the pages together, as shown, to make a booklet. The student writes her name and a title on the booklet's cover. Next, she chooses an adjective from the list and writes the positive, comparative, and superlative forms of the word, each on a separate tab. Then she uses each word in a simple sentence and illustrates the page.

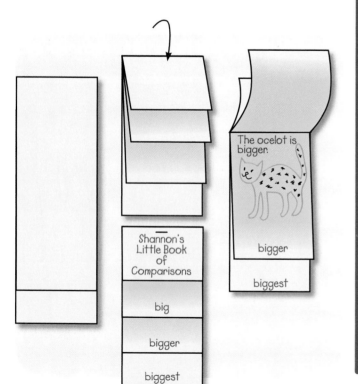

Word Collages

Compound words

Materials:
magazines and newspapers
construction paper (one sheet per child)
scissors
glue

A student searches magazines and newspapers to locate ten or more examples of compound words. He cuts out the words and draws a line to separate the words that make each compound. Then the student glues the words on construction paper and titles his work.

Something in Common

Capitalization

Materials:
copy of page 81
list of capitalization rules
paper

A student reads and sorts the word cards by capitalization rule. She copies each group of words on her paper and then writes the rule that applies to each group.

Always capitalize these words:
- first word in a sentence
- proper names of people, places, and things
- days of the week, months of the year, and holidays
- main words of book and song titles

Casey

August
Thanksgiving
Wednesday
January
Fourth of July
Memorial Day
Sunday
Rule: Capitalize days of the week, months of the year, and holidays.

Stick It to Me

Pronouns

Materials:
sentence strips labeled with sentences
sticky notes labeled with pronouns
paper

A student identifies the subject noun on a sentence strip. He copies the sentence on a sheet of paper and underlines the subject noun (or nouns). Then he replaces the noun with a corresponding sticky-note pronoun. He rereads the sentence, copies it on his paper, and underlines the pronoun. He continues in this manner until each pronoun is used at least once.

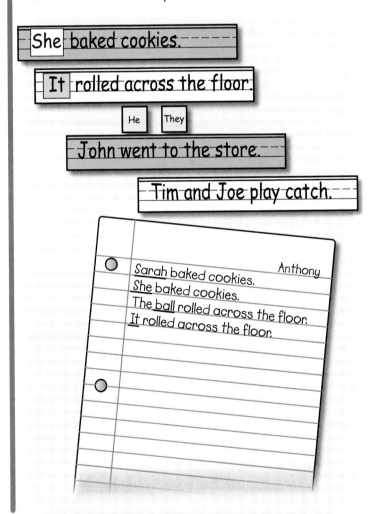

She baked cookies.

It rolled across the floor.

He   They

John went to the store.

Tim and Joe play catch.

Anthony

Sarah baked cookies.
She baked cookies.
The ball rolled across the floor.
It rolled across the floor.

Quite a Pair!

Homophones

Materials:
student copies of the pear patterns on page 82
list of homophones
dictionary
scissors
hole puncher
yarn

Possible homophones include *aunt/ant, blue/blew, chilly/ chili, dough/doe, eight/ate, ferry/fairy, flower/flour, hare/ hair, meet/meat, quartz/quarts, rode/road, steak/stake, tail/ tale, throne/thrown,* and *toe/tow.*

A student cuts out two pear patterns and then copies the words in a homophone pair on opposite sides of a cutout. She uses the dictionary to help her write and draw the meanings for each word. Then the student uses a different homophone pair to complete the other cutout in the same manner. She hole-punches the tops of both pears and ties them together with a length of yarn.

Compare and Connect

Story elements

Materials:
12" x 18" light-colored paper (one sheet per child)
4" x 12" different-colored paper strips (four per child)
glue

After reading two fiction books with a related theme (friendship, honesty, courage, self-esteem, or responsibility), a student folds four different-colored paper strips in half to make flaps and glues each one to a large sheet of paper as shown. She gives her paper a title according to the books' theme and then writes a different story element above each flap. She writes details about the first book on the outside flaps and writes details about the second book on the inside flaps. If time allows, she draws pictures of the books' covers.

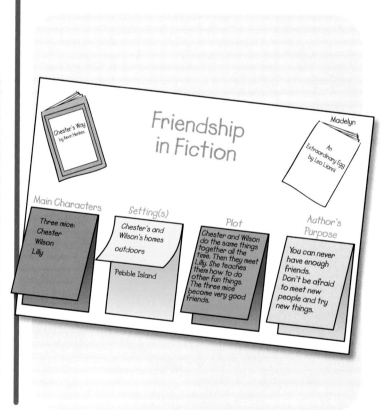

Check, Please!

Spelling

For partners

Materials:
magnetic letters
magnetic surface
list of spelling words
paper

A student calls out a spelling word and his partner spells the word using magnetic letters. The student checks his partner's spelling and keeps a list of any misspelled words on a sheet of paper. After the last word is spelled, he gives the list to his partner to practice at another time. Then the students switch roles and continue practicing in the same manner.

Roll and Write

Paragraph

Materials:
copy of the paragraph prompts on page 82
paragraph outline similar to the one shown
die
paper

A student rolls the die to determine which writing prompt to complete. She uses a paragraph outline like the one shown to create a draft for her paragraph. The student revises the draft and writes her final paragraph at a later time.

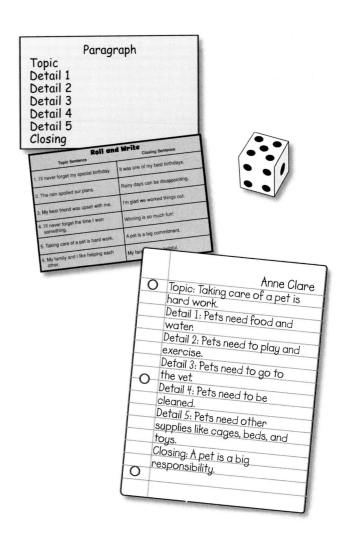

Oh, I Know!

Long vowels

Materials:
copy of the word cards on page 83
craft stick labeled as shown
paper

A student folds a sheet of paper in half, unfolds it, and labels each column as shown. He selects a card and places each end of the craft stick in place of the missing letters to determine whether he can make a word. The student writes the resulting word in the corresponding column. He continues in the same manner until all the cards have been used.

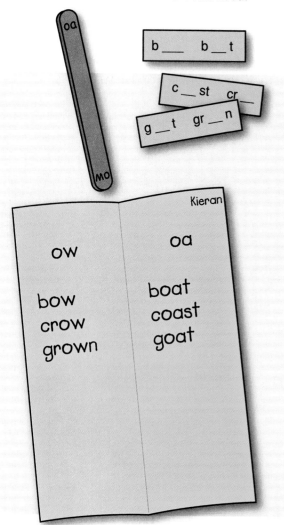

This Sounds Familiar

Multiple-meaning words

Materials:
list of multiple-meaning words
dictionary or dictionary Web site
paper
scissors
crayons

Possible multiple-meaning words include *bank, bark, bat, bowl, dance, fish, hammer, lounge, paint, park, sink, skate, snap, swing, tape, trap, wash,* and *watch.*

A student places a sheet of paper lengthwise on her workspace and folds the two ends toward the center so they are about two inches apart. She unfolds the paper, folds it lengthwise twice, and then unfolds it. The student repositions the side flaps and cuts along each fold line to make flaps. The student chooses four multiple-meaning words and writes each word between the flaps. She draws on each flap a different picture for the meanings of each word. Then she writes the multiple meanings and the parts of speech inside the flaps.

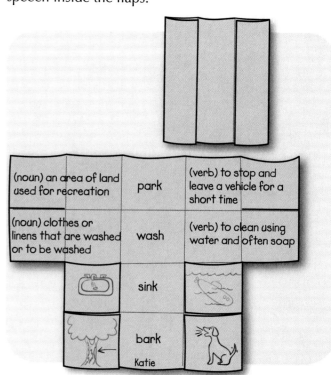

What Fits?

Guide words

Materials:
sentence strips labeled with guide words
index cards labeled with spelling words
paper

A student chooses a sentence strip and places an appropriate index card between the guide words. She copies the three words on her paper and continues in the same manner until all the words have been matched with the appropriate guide words.

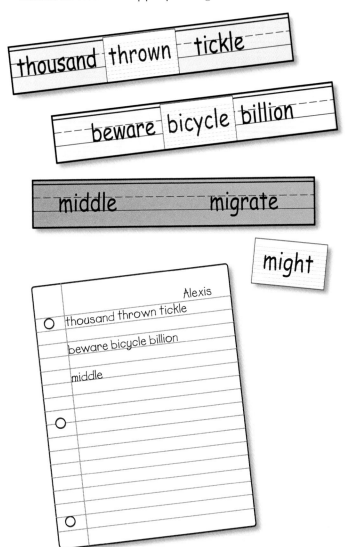

What's for Lunch?

Descriptive writing

Materials:
tagboard copy of the lunchbox pattern on page 83
magazines
construction paper (one sheet per child)
scissors
glue

A student folds a sheet of construction paper in half and traces the lunchbox template on the fold. He cuts through both layers of paper, keeping the fold intact. Then he cuts out a magazine picture of his favorite food, glues it inside the lunchbox, and writes the food's name below it. On the front of the lunchbox the student writes his name and descriptive words about the food without giving its name. He opens the lunchbox and writes a paragraph about his favorite food using the descriptive words.

watermelon

Watermelon is one of my favorite foods. It is sweet and juicy. The outside is green and hard. The inside is red, soft, and seedy. Watermelon is cool and refreshing to eat on a hot summer day. I like eating it by the slice.

Add -s or -es

Plural nouns

Materials:
copy of the picture cards on page 84, cut apart
paper

A student reads each card and writes the plural form of the word on his paper. Then he uses the word in a sentence and underlines the plural noun.

puzzle

paintbrush

pencil

Ben

My mother bought new pencils for me.

Mike and I like building puzzles during indoor recess.

Truth or Notion

Fact and opinion

Materials:
paper
scissors
stapler
crayons

After reading a nonfiction book, a student cuts a sheet of paper in half lengthwise, folds the two pieces in half, and staples the paper together to make a mini-book. She writes on the cover a title and draws a picture that reflects the topic of her book. The student opens the book and then writes and illustrates a fact on the left page and an opinion on the right page. She repeats the process two more times to complete her book.

Fact: The slant-faced grasshopper rubs its hind legs across its front wings to make music.

Opinion: Grasshoppers make beautiful music with their legs and wings.

Garden Insects
A Fact and Opinion Minibook

Madison

"Wheel-ly" Cool Nouns

Nouns

Materials:
student copies of the wheel pattern on page 84
independent reading book
paper
pen

A student copies ten sentences from an independent reading book on his paper and then circles the nouns in each sentence. He writes "c" above each common noun and "p" above each proper noun. Then the student writes each noun in the appropriate section of the wheel.

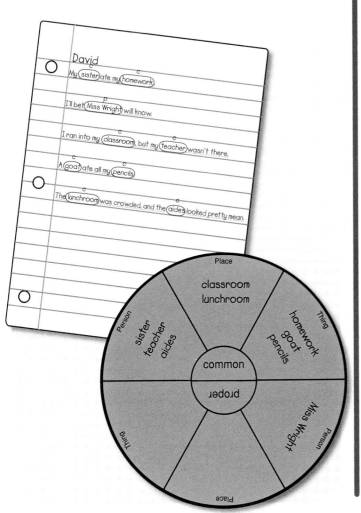

"Wow" Words

Word choice

Materials:
list of blah words
small binder ring (one per student)
index cards (two per student)
thesaurus
hole puncher

Possible blah words include *bad, big, boy, cold, fast, girl, good, happy, hard, hot, little, look, mad, mean, new, nice, old, pretty, sad, slow, soft, start, stop,* and *ugly.*

A student selects a blah word from the list. She uses the thesaurus to find an interesting synonym ("wow" word) for the blah word. The student writes both words on an index card; then she uses the "wow" word in a sentence. The student chooses another blah word and continues in the same manner. Then she hole-punches her completed index cards and inserts a binder ring.

Vowel Teams

Long vowels

Materials:
2 copies of the jersey pattern on page 85,
 cut out and labeled as shown
copy of the word cards on page 85, cut apart
paper

A student reads a word card and matches it to the jersey with the appropriate vowel pair. He continues in this manner until all cards have been placed on a jersey. Then the student folds a sheet of paper in half, unfolds it, and labels each column with a vowel pair. He refers to the cards to list each word in the appropriate column.

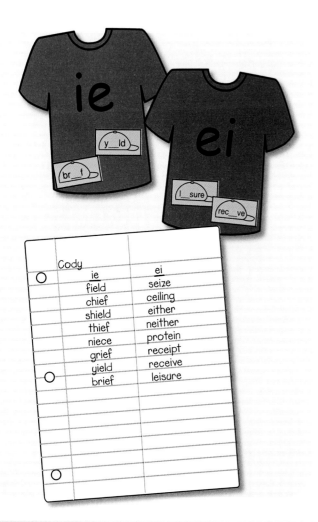

On the Lookout!

Suffixes

Materials:
list of suffixes, similar to the one shown
magazine or newspaper articles placed in sheet protectors
dry-erase marker
paper towel
paper

A student uses a dry-erase marker to circle all the words with suffixes she can find in an article. She copies the words on her paper and writes a brief definition alongside each word. Then the student erases the circles, selects a new page, and continues in the same manner.

Candid Compositions

Editing

For partners

Materials:
candid photographs or magazine
    pictures (one per student pair)
sticky notes
construction paper (one per student pair)
paper
scissors
glue

A pair of students chooses one photograph. Each student writes a vivid description of what's happening in the photo. Next, the partners swap paragraphs and read each other's work. Each student writes on a sticky note no more than three questions to guide his partner about any missing details. Then the student returns the paragraph and sticky note to his partner. Each student makes the necessary corrections to his final draft. The pair cuts out the paragraphs and then mounts the photo and paragraphs on a sheet of construction paper.

Ronan

Sleigh Ride
How fast did they go?
How cold was it?
How big was the hill?

Griffin

Fun in the Snow
What was the color of the sled?
How did snow feel on the kids' faces?
How many rode on the sled?

Take a Spin!

Capitalization

Materials:
map of the United States
spinner labeled as shown
paper clip
paper

A student divides a sheet of paper into four columns and labels each column with a term from the spinner. She uses the paper clip and her pencil to spin the spinner and then locates a corresponding example on the map. The student writes the example in the matching column and underlines each capital letter. She repeats the process in the same manner as time allows.

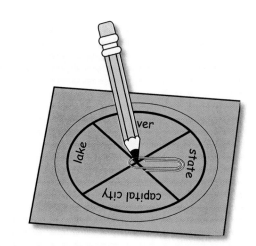

Kara			
State	Capital City	Lake	River
Hawaii	Sacramento	Lake Superior	Mississippi River

Apostrophe Alert

Possessive nouns

Materials:
copy of the noun cards on page 86, cut apart
2 cards labeled with apostrophe rules as shown
paper

A student reads the rules and sorts the noun cards into singular possessive and plural possessive groups. Next, she folds a sheet of paper in half, unfolds it, and labels each column as shown. Then the student copies the possessive nouns in the appropriate columns.

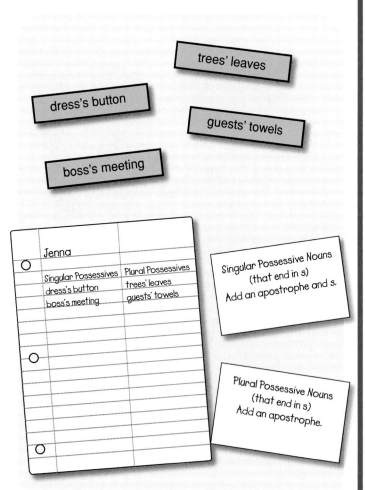

trees' leaves

dress's button

guests' towels

boss's meeting

Jenna

Singular Possessives	Plural Possessives
dress's button	trees' leaves
boss's meeting	guests' towels

Singular Possessive Nouns
(that end in s)
Add an apostrophe and s.

Plural Possessive Nouns
(that end in s)
Add an apostrophe.

Then What Happened?

Predictions

Materials:
several comic strips, cut in half and labeled "beginning" or "ending"
2 envelopes labeled as shown
index cards

A student reads the first half of a comic strip from the envelope labeled "beginning." Then he draws a detailed prediction of the comic's ending on an index card. He locates and removes the comic's actual ending from the envelope labeled "ending" and compares it with his prediction. The student returns the comic strips to the appropriate envelopes and continues in the same manner as time permits.

beginning

Roxy says you talk to acorns.

To what?

To acorns!

She's silly! Tell Roxy that I said...

ending

Oh, there!

...that I think she's nuts!

I think she's nuts! Me... talking to acorns? Ridiculous!

Derek

It's a Match!

Contractions

Materials:
index cards labeled with contractions
and their matching word pairs

For partners

Partners shuffle the index cards, take seven cards each, and stack the remaining cards facedown. Each player sets aside any matching cards. Then Player 1 asks Player 2 for a contraction or a contraction's matching word pair. If Player 2 has the card, he hands it to Player 1. If not, he tells Player 1 to choose a card from the deck. If Player 1 draws a card from the pile and makes a contraction match, she says, "It's a match!" She then takes another turn. If a match is not made, her turn ends and Player 2 takes his turn. Play continues until all matches are made. The player with more sets wins.

Stuck on Cursive

Cursive

Materials:
laminated sentence strips, each with
a sticker of a different image
dry-erase marker
paper towel

A student selects a sentence strip, names the sticker, and writes the word several times in cursive. Then she selects a new strip and continues in the same manner. When she's finished, she wipes her strips clean with a paper towel.

Set 12

It's a Toss-Up

Digraphs

Materials:
copy of the cube pattern on page 87, labeled
  with different digraphs and assembled
copy of the cube pattern on page 87, labeled
  with 1s and 2s and assembled
paper

Possible digraphs include *ch, ph, sh, th, wh, kn, sn, fl, gl,
pl, sl, dr, tr,* and *sp.*

A student divides her paper into six columns and labels each column with a different digraph from the cube. The student rolls both cubes and then names a word that begins with the digraph rolled and has the number of syllables that appears on the number cube. She writes the word and its number of syllables in the appropriate section. The student continues in the same manner until a desired number of words are recorded.

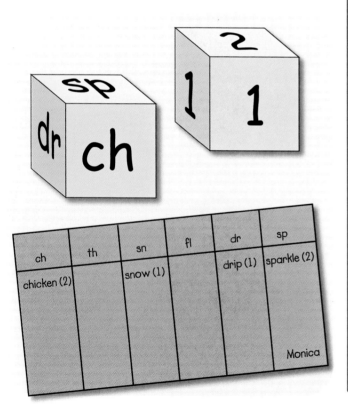

Spot the Imposter

Synonyms and antonyms

Materials:
5 copies of the magnifying glass patterns on page 87,
  each cut out and labeled with a synonym or
  an antonym pair plus one extra word
10 craft sticks, each labeled with a different
  number from 1 through 10, taped to the
  magnifying glass cutouts
paper

A student divides his paper into three columns and labels each column as shown. He numbers his paper from 1 to 10. Then the student reads the words on a magnifying glass and names the synonym or antonym pair. He writes the word pair on his paper next to the corresponding number and records the imposter. He continues in the same manner until all ten magnifying glasses are completed.

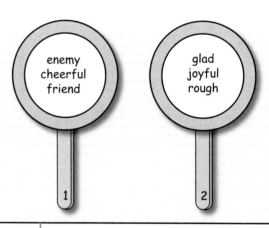

Gavin

	Synonyms	Antonyms	Imposter
1.		enemy/friend	cheerful
2.	glad/joyful		rough
3.			

Book in Bloom

Main idea and details

Materials:
paper
colored pencils

After reading a story, a student draws a flower as shown. He writes the book's title on the flower's stem and the author's name on the leaf. The student writes the story's main idea in the flower's center and the supporting details on the petals.

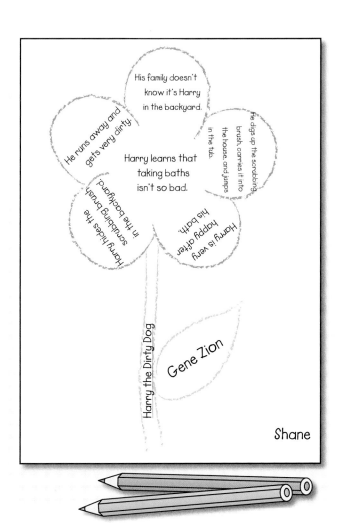

Get the Meaning

Dictionary

Materials:
magazines or catalogs
small binder rings (one per child)
large index cards (at least three per child)
dictionary
scissors
glue
hole puncher

A student cuts out a small magazine or catalog picture and glues it in the corner of an index card. She uses the dictionary to help her write on the index card the page number, guide words, spelling, and definition of the word. The student continues in the same manner to complete at least two more cards. Then she hole-punches the cards and binds them together with a ring.

Dialing Up Words

Digraphs

Materials:
2 card stock strips secured with a brad to a paper
    plate, strips and plate labeled as shown
paper
dictionary

A student folds a sheet of paper in half, unfolds
it, and labels each column with one of the digraphs
shown. Next, he turns one of the digraph strips to a
word part on the plate. If the student thinks he has
made a real word, he writes it on his paper in the
appropriate column. Then the student repeats the
process with the other digraph strip. He continues
in this manner for each word part. Then he uses the
dictionary to check his list of words.

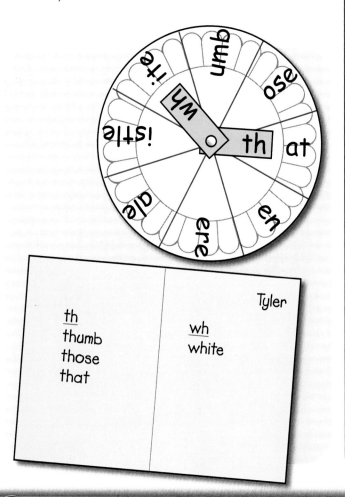

Deducing Detectives

Inferences

Materials:
envelopes labeled with the nursery rhyme titles shown
copy of the picture cards on page 88, cut apart and placed
    in the corresponding envelopes
paper

A student selects an envelope, removes the picture
cards, and arranges them in numerical order. She
reads each card's question and uses the picture to
make an inference. The student writes the nursery
rhyme title on her paper and answers each question.
She returns the cards to the envelope and repeats the
process with another envelope as time permits.

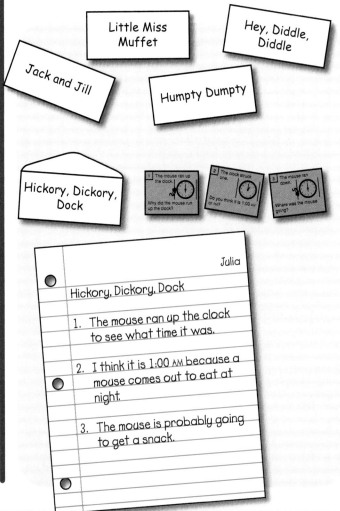

Water Words

Spelling

Materials:
list of spelling words
chalkboard
cup of water
paintbrush

A student dips the paintbrush in water and then "paints" each spelling word on the chalkboard.

snowflake
icicle
frost
sleigh
blizzard
igloo

How Do You Feel?

Thesaurus

Materials:
1" x 8" construction paper strips (five per child)
list of feeling words, like the one shown
thesaurus
markers
glue

A student chooses a feeling word from the list and uses a marker to write it on the left side of a paper strip. She locates the word in the thesaurus and writes two or three synonyms on her strip. Next, the student puts glue on the right side of the paper strip and attaches it to the left side to form a loop. Then she repeats the process with a different word and another strip but links this strip to the first paper loop to form a chain. The student continues in this manner until a predetermined number of links have been made.

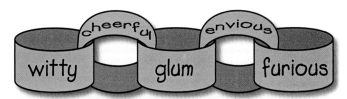

cheerful
envious
witty
glum
furious

shy   bashful   coy

Feeling Words

happy	shy
mad	smart
sad	honest
scared	nice
lazy	calm
tired	jealous
proud	cruel
worried	

Put Into Words

Double consonants

Materials:
copy of the letter cards on page 89, cut apart
paper

A student manipulates three cards at a time to create a word that contains a double consonant. Each time a new word is created, he writes it on his paper. When he is satisfied with his list, he divides each word on his paper into syllables.

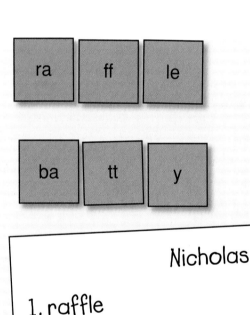

Word Series Flipbook

ABC order to the third letter

Materials:
index cards, each labeled with a list of five words that have the same two beginning letters
sentence strips (one per child)
sticky notes (four per child)
stapler

A student selects an index card, determines which word from the list is last in alphabetical order, and writes the word on the sentence strip. Next, the student chooses another word from the list and writes on a sticky note all its letters except the first two. She repeats the process for the remaining words on the list and then stacks the sticky notes so they are in alphabetical order from top to bottom. She places the stack of sticky notes on top of the word on the sentence strip so only its first two letters are showing. Then she staples the sticky notes to the sentence strip to form a flipbook.

Double-Sided Bookmark

Homophones

Materials:
list of homophones
2" x 6" tagboard strip (one per child)
12" length of yarn (one per child)
hole puncher
crayons

A student chooses a pair of homophones from the list, uses both in a sentence on one side of her strip, and illustrates the sentence. Then the student turns the strip over to write and illustrate another sentence that contains a different pair of homophones. She punches a hole at the top of the strip, threads the yarn through the hole, and ties a knot to complete her bookmark.

"I'll be happy to walk you down the aisle when the time comes!" said my dad.

Please don't bury my berry!

Natalia

Homophones
whale	wail
bury	berry
flea	flee
hoarse	horse
sale	sail
I'll	aisle
mousse	moose
see	sea
tale	tail
aunt	ant

Robust Writing

Combining sentences

Materials:
copy of the sentence cards on page 89, cut apart
paper

A student numbers his paper from one to six. He reads the sentences on the first card and determines a way to combine them, making sure the number of words in the combined sentence equals the number of blank spaces on the strip. The student writes the resulting sentence on his paper and continues in this manner until he has written all six combined sentences.

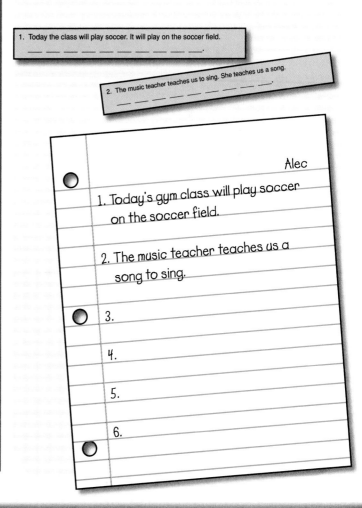

1. Today the class will play soccer. It will play on the soccer field.
___ ___ ___ ___ ___ ___ ___ ___ ___.

2. The music teacher teaches us to sing. She teaches us a song.
___ ___ ___ ___ ___ ___ ___ ___.

Alec

1. Today's gym class will play soccer on the soccer field.

2. The music teacher teaches us a song to sing.

3.

4.

5.

6.

Seen But Not Heard

Silent letters

Materials:
copy of the picture cards on page 90, cut apart
paper

A student divides his paper into four columns and labels each column as shown. He selects a picture card, chooses the correct spelling of the word that matches the picture, and writes the word in the appropriate column. Then he underlines on his paper each word's silent letter or letters. The student continues in the same manner until he has listed all the words.

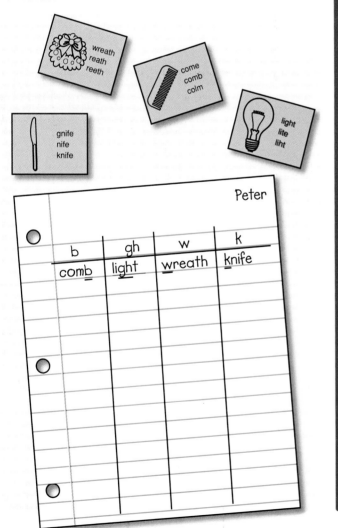

Notable Nouns

Capitalization

Materials:
copy of the picture cards on page 91, cut apart
paper

A student selects four cards and arranges them to make a 2 x 2 square on her workspace. Next, the student folds a sheet of paper to make four sections, unfolds the paper, and writes the name of the holiday or special event each picture represents in the corresponding section. Then the student uses each name in a sentence, being sure to correctly capitalize her work. If time allows, she draws an illustration for each sentence.

Tell-All Tents

Summarizing

Materials:
index cards (four per child)
tape
crayons
scissors

After reading a book, a student turns three index cards vertically and writes on one card the title of the book, the author's name, and a few sentences about the story's beginning. He writes on another card sentences about the story's middle and writes on the third card sentences about the story's end. Then he tapes the three cards together in sequential order and tapes the two free ends together to form a tent. Finally, on the fourth card, the student draws and cuts out an image that symbolizes the book and tapes it inside the tent.

Quite the Character

Character description

Materials:
paper

A student folds down the top three inches of his paper to create a flap. With the flap down, he draws on the front of his paper the character's face and then writes the character's name under the flap. Then he lists on the back of his paper clues about the character's physical description and the story. He also includes the corresponding page numbers where the clues can be verified.

Related Actions

Cause and effect

Materials:
copies of the recording sheet on page 91 (one per student)

A student observes the teacher or other students in the classroom engaged in an activity such as proofreading, erasing the board, or sharpening a pencil. He writes his observation under the "Cause" heading on the chart. Then the student writes a result of the action under the "Effect" heading. He repeats the process two more times to complete the chart.

Name **Evan**   Recording sheet

On the Lookout

Cause (What Do I See?)	Effect (What Might Happen?)
1. Vito reads his library book in the reading corner.	He will be able to start his book report.
2. Angelina gives a pencil to Cohen.	Cohen can finish his seatwork.
3. Ms. Smith helps James with his math worksheet.	James will get better at multiplication.

Homonymous Headlines

Multiple-meaning words

Materials:
copy of the headline list on the top of page 91
dictionary
paper

A student folds a sheet of paper in half and unfolds it. He copies at the top of his paper one of the headlines from the list and underlines the word that implies multiple meanings. Next, the student uses the dictionary to write two different definitions for the word that could possibly explain the headline's meaning; then he draws a picture for each. He draws a star next to the definition that makes the headline seem realistic and a smiley face next to the definition that makes the headline seem ridiculous.

Strange Object Found in Brush

short trees or shrubs of poor quality ☆

a tool made of bristles used for cleaning, smoothing, or painting ☺

Zachary

Cold Season Starts Early
Family Seal Found After 100 Years
Police Officer Takes a Bite Out of Crime
Bank Teller Complains About Change
Baseball Player Steals Home
Golfer Drives Ball Over 250 Yards
Mother Finds Baby in the Nursery
Young Teen Becomes a Star
Local Artist Draws a Crowd
Strange Object Found in Brush

Spot Check

Text-to-self connections

Materials:
chapter book
paper

A student writes the book's title and chapter on his paper. He draws three large circles (spots) and labels each one as shown. After reading the chapter, the student stops to complete each spot. In the first spot, he writes about something he is reminded of as he reads. In the second spot, the student writes something he understands about a particular character or situation. In the third spot, he writes how he would react or feel if he were a character in the book.

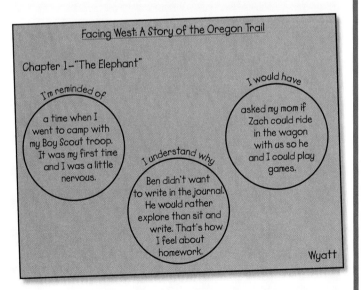

Word Order

Different sentence beginnings

Materials:
list of sentences and the color code shown,
    placed together in a plastic sheet protector
3 dry-erase markers (blue, red, green)
paper

A student refers to the color code and reads the first sentence. She uses a blue dry-erase marker to underline the words that answer the question "Where?" Next, she underlines in red and green, respectively, the answers to the questions "Did what?" and "Who or what?" Then, on her paper, the student rewrites the sentence, changing the word order. To do this, she begins the new sentence with the "Where?" phrase followed by the "Who or what?" phrase, and completes the sentence with the "Did what?" phrase. The student continues in this same manner until a predetermined number of sentences have been rewritten.

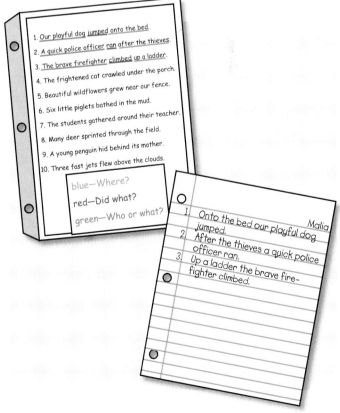

Follow the Rules

Adding -ed

Materials:
sentence strips labeled as shown
index card, folded and labeled as shown
list of rules like the one shown
paper

A student folds a sheet of paper in half, unfolds it, and labels each column as shown. He places the folded index card over the top of a sentence strip, slides it to the end of the word, and then turns the folded index card around to test which rule applies to the word. He writes the word with its correct ending in the appropriate column. The student continues in this manner until a desired number of words are listed on his paper.

	Andres
Change y to i	No change
carried	stayed
cried	enjoyed
buried	obeyed
supplied	destroyed
replied	played

Final-y Rules
- Change the y to i if a word ends with a <u>consonant</u> followed by y.
- Do not change y to i if a word ends with a <u>vowel</u> followed by y.

play ed   play ied

carry   bury

cry   stay

Could You Believe It?

Fiction and nonfiction

Materials:
student copies of page 92
collection of fables or folktales

After a student reads a fable or folktale, she writes in the top middle box on her recording sheet an event that has both believable and unbelievable elements. In the cloud to the left of the box, she writes a reason why the event is unbelievable. In the book to the right of the box, she writes a reason why the event is believable. The student continues in the same manner with three more events.

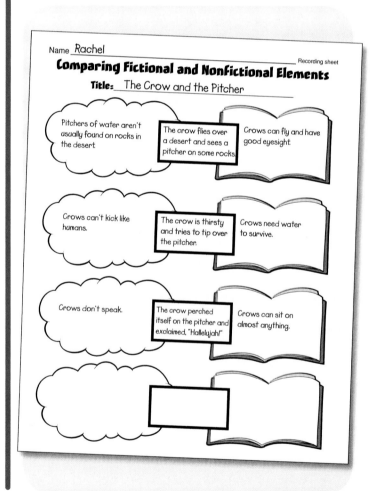

Name **Rachel**

Recording sheet
Comparing Fictional and Nonfictional Elements
Title: **The Crow and the Pitcher**

Pitchers of water aren't usually found on rocks in the desert.

The crow flies over a desert and sees a pitcher on some rocks.

Crows can fly and have good eyesight.

Crows can't kick like humans.

The crow is thirsty and tries to tip over the pitcher.

Crows need water to survive.

Crows don't speak.

The crow perched itself on the pitcher and exclaimed, "Hallelujah!"

Crows can sit on almost anything.

Regular or Irregular

Verbs

Materials:
paper
list of verb rules

A student folds a sheet of paper in half, unfolds it, and labels each column with the headings shown. He skims a book to find a minimum of 12 different verbs. The student writes and underlines each verb under the appropriate column heading. Then he writes either the present or past tense form of each underlined verb.

Regular Verbs—Add *-ed* to regular present-tense verbs to form the past tense.

Irregular Verbs—For most present-tense irregular verbs, the word changes to form the past tense.

Kyle

Regular Verbs		Irregular Verbs	
present	past	present	past
want	wanted	sit	sat
ask	asked	think	thought
smile	smiled	give	gave

Word for Word

Cursive

Materials:
sentence strips, programmed with idioms written in cursive
small sticky notes
paper

A student copies on her paper each idiom, skipping a few lines between each one. If time allows, she draws the literal meaning of each expression on a sticky note and places each note next to its corresponding sentence.

Make the Connection

Consonant clusters

Materials:
copy of the cube pattern on page 87,
  labeled as shown
copy of the gameboard on page 93
  (one per student pair)
2 different-colored crayons

For partners

Player 1 rolls the cube and decides if the cluster rolled can be added to a word part on the gameboard to make a word. If it can, the student writes the cluster on the appropriate space on the gameboard using a crayon, and Player 2 takes a turn. If Player 1 cannot make a word, his turn is over, and Player 2 takes her turn using the other color of crayon to write. When a player makes three words in a row or column that begin with the same consonant cluster, he draws a connecting line through all three squares and scores a tally mark. Play continues until all the squares are filled. The player with the most tally marks wins.

Player 1 Score		Connect 3			Player 2 Score	
een	scrub	ap	straw	stretch	street
eam	scratch	inkle	ead	out	ong
ape	scrunch	ut	ipe	ide	uggle
oll	ess	ike	ing	ain	ay

Classroom Manuals

Writing directions

Materials:
list of time-order words
paper

Possible time-order words include *first, next, then, after that,* and *finally.*

A student brainstorms a list of four steps to complete a classroom procedure, such as making lunch choices, lining up, or packing up at dismissal time. Next, she folds a sheet of paper in half horizontally and then folds it in half vertically twice. She unfolds the vertical folds. Then she cuts along the top layer's fold lines to make four flaps as shown. The student draws on each flap a step of the procedure, keeping her illustrations in sequential order. Then she lifts each flap and writes directions for each step using time-order words.

Read, Sort, Write

Verb tenses

Materials:
cards, labeled as shown
sentence strips, labeled as shown
paper

A student arranges the cards on a flat surface and then reads a sentence strip. He places the sentence strip below the card that corresponds with the underlined verb or verbs in the sentence. The student continues to sort each sentence according to its verb tense. Then he labels his paper with the verb tenses shown on the cards and records each verb in the appropriate column.

Present

The girl gives the puppy a bath.

He shakes the water off.

Past

She dried him with a towel.

The puppy licked his wet fur.

Future

The puppy will jump out of the tub.

Next time, the puppy will hide from the girl.

The Replace Race

Prefixes

For partners

Materials:
copy of page 94 (one per student pair)
game markers (one per child)
coin

Students follow the directions on the gameboard and alternate play until one player reaches the finish line.

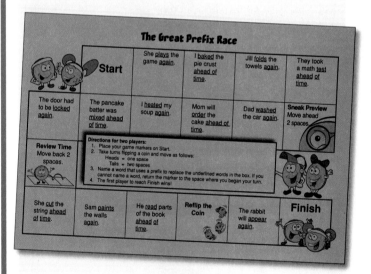

Odd Word Out

Dictionary

Materials:
cards, numbered and programmed
   like the ones shown
dictionary
paper

A student selects a card and uses the dictionary to determine which listed word is different in meaning from the other two. He writes on his paper the index card's number and the word that doesn't belong. The student continues in the same manner until he has identified a predetermined number of words.

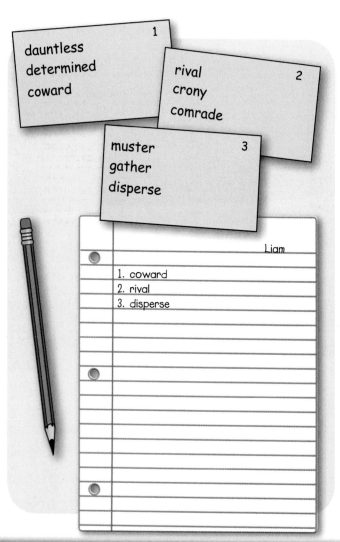

```
1
dauntless
determined
coward
```

```
2
rival
crony
comrade
```

```
3
muster
gather
disperse
```

Liam

1. coward
2. rival
3. disperse

Communicating Ideas

Summarizing

Materials:
student copies of the cell phone pattern on page 93
3" x 9" construction paper (one per child)
scissors
glue

After reading a story, a student cuts out a copy of the cell phone pattern and writes the title of the book and the author's name on the cell phone's screen. Next, she folds a sheet of construction paper in half and turns it so the fold is at the top. She glues the cell phone pattern to the paper, aligning the top of the phone with the fold. Then she lifts the flap and writes brief details about the book, as shown.

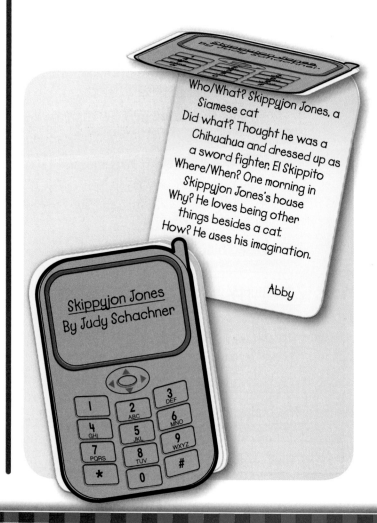

Who/What? Skippyjon Jones, a Siamese cat
Did what? Thought he was a Chihuahua and dressed up as a sword fighter, El Skippito
Where/When? One morning in Skippyjon Jones's house
Why? He loves being other things besides a cat.
How? He uses his imagination.

Abby

Skippyjon Jones
By Judy Schachner

Sentence Builders

Subject-verb agreement

Materials:
copy of the task card on page 93
newspapers and magazines
paper
scissors
glue

A student reads the directions for the first task. He writes the task's number on his paper, cuts from newspapers or magazines words that match the task, and glues the words on his paper. Then he completes the task by writing sentences on his paper as directed. He continues in this manner with the remaining tasks.

Tasks

1. Cut out three present-tense verbs. Use each verb in a different sentence.

2. Cut out two proper nouns and one verb. Use all three words in one sentence.

3. Cut out one present-tense verb. Use the present-tense verb in a sentence. Then rewrite the sentence in past tense.

1. **finds** drives **bring**

Sara finds her cat in the tree.
My father drives me to school in the morning.
I bring my lunch to school every day.

David

Back of the Book

Glossary

Materials:
copy of the cube pattern on page 87, each face labeled with a different letter, assembled as shown
several books with glossaries
paper

A student divides her paper into six columns and labels each one as shown. She rolls the cube and writes the letter rolled in the appropriate column on her paper. Next, she turns to the corresponding glossary pages in a book and completes each remaining column on her paper. Then the student rolls the cube again. If she rolls the same letter, she uses the glossary of a different book to complete each column. She continues in this manner as time allows.

Book Title	Letter	Number of Entries	The Longest Entry	The Shortest Entry	A Word I Don't Know
Weather	C	3	condensation	cloud	current
Hurricanes	E	4	evacuate	eye	eyewall
Your Environment	S	4	short-wave energy	sediment	symbiotic

What's the Objective?

Author's purpose

Materials:
children's magazine articles with the titles
removed, cut out and numbered
paper

A student reads an article and then writes its number on his paper. Next to the number, the student writes the author's purpose—to inform, to entertain, or to give directions—for writing the article. Then he selects another article and repeats the process. As an added challenge, the student writes a title for each article.

Matthew

1. to inform–Exciting New Discovery

2. to give directions–How to Make a Halloween Costume

3. to entertain

See It Their Way

Point of view

Materials:
independent reading book
paper

A student writes on her paper the title and author's name of a recently read book. She selects a conflict that involves the main character and writes a sentence about the conflict. Next, she draws a picture of the character under a thought bubble. Inside the bubble, the student writes what the character is thinking or feeling at the time of the conflict. Then she draws the other characters that are involved with the conflict and writes their thoughts and feelings in separate thought bubbles.

Clear and Concise

Commas

Materials:
sentence strips, labeled similar to the ones shown
transparency sheet cut into small pieces,
    each piece labeled with a comma, as shown
paper clips
paper

A student selects a sentence strip and determines if a comma is needed before or after the dialogue. Then he appropriately positions a comma on top of the sentence strip. He secures the comma with a paper clip and then copies the correctly punctuated sentence onto his paper. He continues in this manner with each remaining sentence strip.

"I'm very sleepy," Goldilocks said.

The team cheered, "Hip hip hooray!"

,

Nathan

"I'm very sleepy," Goldilocks said.
The team cheered, "Hip hip hooray!"

Sketch a Tale

Story mapping

Materials:
student copies of page 95
paper

A student writes on her story map words or phrases that describe elements of her story. Then, on a sheet of paper, the student compiles her ideas to write her first draft.

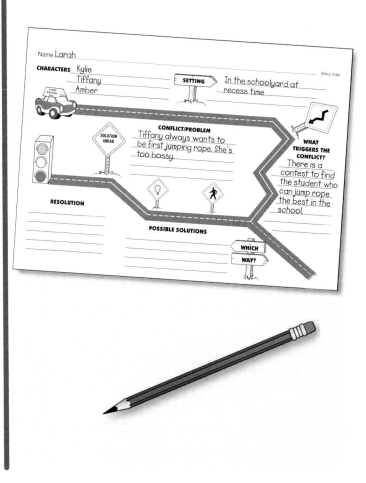

Name Larah

CHARACTERS Kylie
Tiffany
Amber

SETTING In the schoolyard at recess time

CONFLICT/PROBLEM
Tiffany always wants to be first jumping rope. She's too bossy.

WHAT TRIGGERS THE CONFLICT?
There is a contest to find the student who can jump rope the best in the school.

SOLUTION AHEAD

RESOLUTION

POSSIBLE SOLUTIONS

WHICH WAY?

Story map

Two-Sided Statements

Fact and opinion

Materials:
magazines and sales circulars
paper
scissors
glue

A child cuts from a magazine or circular a picture of something he likes and glues the picture to a sheet of paper. Next, he writes two facts and two opinions below the picture. If time allows, he turns his paper over and repeats the process using a picture of something he dislikes.

Fact
Ice cream is a dairy product.
Ice cream is a frozen food.

Opinion
Chocolate ice cream is better than vanilla.
Ice cream is the best dessert on the planet!

Trevor

Stick to It

Capitalization

Materials:
books or student magazines
list of capitalization rules, like the one shown
sticky notes (one for each rule per child)
paper

A student writes each rule on a separate sticky note and then places the notes on a sheet of paper. He reviews a book or magazine to find an example of each rule. When he finds one, he flips up the corresponding sticky note and copies the example onto the paper.

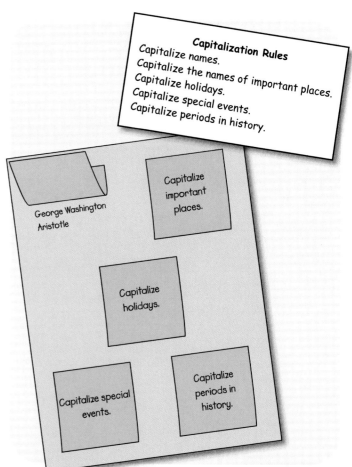

Capitalization Rules
Capitalize names.
Capitalize the names of important places.
Capitalize holidays.
Capitalize special events.
Capitalize periods in history.

George Washington
Aristotle

Capitalize important places.

Capitalize holidays.

Capitalize special events.

Capitalize periods in history.

Review a Reading

Generating and answering questions

For partners

Materials:
paper

A child draws a large *w* on her paper, like the one shown. She writes along each line a question about a recent class reading, being sure to start each question with the letter *w*. Then she swaps papers with a partner who answers each question under its line.

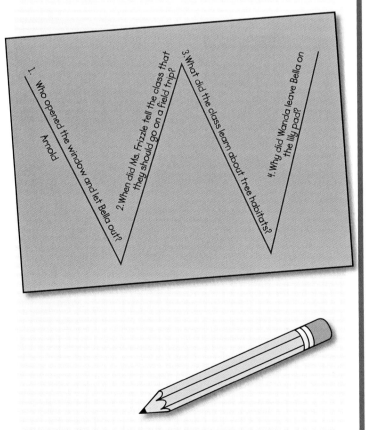

1. Who opened the window and let Bella out?
Arnold
2. When did Ms. Frizzle tell the class that they should go on a field trip?
3. What did the class learn about tree habitats?
4. Why did Wanda leave Bella on the lily pad?

Looking for Variety

Writing reference

Materials:
familiar books
index cards (one per child)
craft sticks (one per child)
scissors
glue
paper

A student folds her index card in half and cuts out a small rectangle along the fold. She unfolds the card and glues it to a craft stick to make a viewfinder. Next, the student uses the viewfinder to guide her reading as she reviews the sentences in a familiar story. Each time she finds a sentence that begins in an interesting manner, she writes it on a sheet of paper. She continues until she has recorded a predetermined number of sentences. Then, when she has a writing assignment, the student uses her list to find different ways to start her sentences.

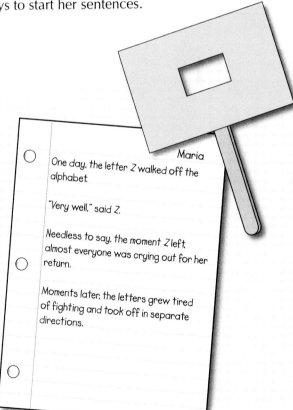

Maria

One day, the letter Z walked off the alphabet.

"Very well," said Z.

Needless to say, the moment Z left, almost everyone was crying out for her return.

Moments later, the letters grew tired of fighting and took off in separate directions.

Roll and Respond

Character analysis

Materials:
question card from page 96
die
paper

After reading a fictional story, a child rolls the die and reads the matching-numbered question. Then he writes the number of the question on his paper and records his response.

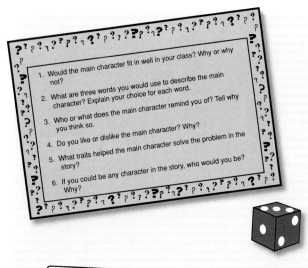

1. Would the main character fit in well in your class? Why or why not?

2. What are three words you would use to describe the main character? Explain your choice for each word.

3. Who or what does the main character remind you of? Tell why you think so.

4. Do you like or dislike the main character? Why?

5. What traits helped the main character solve the problem in the story?

6. If you could be any character in the story, who would you be? Why?

Jacob

6. If I could be any character, I would be Dr. De Soto's wife. Dr. De Soto was very popular with the big animals, so they would like her too. Also, Mrs. De Soto was smart enough to make a plan so the fox would not eat either of them.

Revealing Clues

ABC order to the third letter

Materials:
list of word sets like the ones shown
1" paper strips
paper

A student chooses a word set and writes each word on a separate paper strip. She folds the first two letters of each word back behind the strip. Then she uses the third letter to order the strips alphabetically, unfolds each strip to reveal the whole word, and writes each word on her paper. She continues with another word set as time allows.

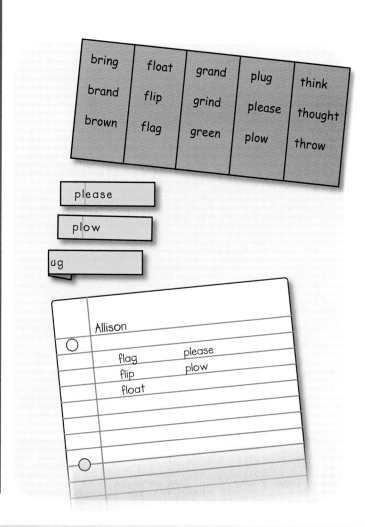

bring	float	grand	plug	think
brand	flip	grind	please	thought
brown	flag	green	plow	throw

please

plow

ug

Allison

flag   please
flip   plow
float

Pretend Pen Pal

Letter writing

Materials:
paper

A student assumes the role of a citizen of a recently studied community or time period. She writes a letter to another student in her class, giving information about the chosen place or historical period.

February 9, 1860

Dear Jordan,
Hi! My name is Mo and I also live in Cleveland. But I am writing this letter from the 1800s. A lot of exciting things have happened around here in recent years. New forms of transportation have helped us grow. First, the Erie Canal linked this city to the Atlantic Ocean. Then there was the first steamboat on Lake Erie. Both of these things helped with trading goods. Then we got railroads. Now there are so many people living and working here!
Thank you for letting me share a little bit of what's happening around here.

Your new friend,
Mo

Now You're Talking!

Quotation marks

Materials:
student copies of page 97
scissors
stapler

A child reflects on a conversation he recently had. He writes one related dialogue sentence on each mouth card, writing the spoken words across the mouth with appropriate punctuation and the rest of the sentence outside the mouth. When he has written all four sentences, he cuts apart the cards and staples them in order.

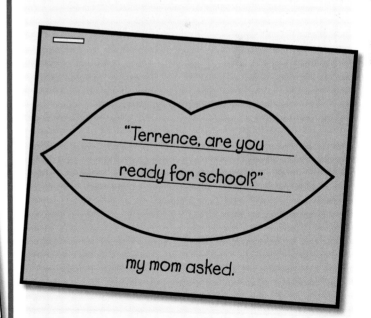

"Terrence, are you ready for school?"

my mom asked.

Showing Ownership

Possessive nouns

Materials:
cards from the top of page 98, copied
    on tagboard and cut apart
paper

A child folds a sheet of paper in half, unfolds it, and writes each noun in the left column. He places an appropriate apostrophe card next to each noun card and then writes each possessive noun in the right-hand column.

moms   '

farmer	farmer's
boy	boy's
baker	baker's
coach	coach's
cats	cats'
moms	
doctors	
partners	
men	
children	

Noah

Making Choices

Following written directions

Materials:
copy of the directions cards from the bottom
    of page 98, cut apart
paper

A child reads the directions on each of the cards and determines which set would be the best one to follow. She writes her choice on her paper and then records her reasons for choosing it.

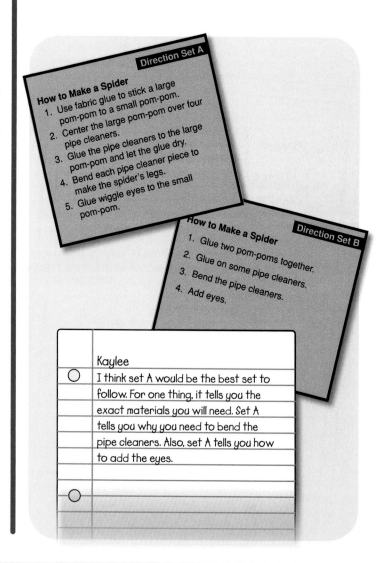

Direction Set A

How to Make a Spider
1. Use fabric glue to stick a large pom-pom to a small pom-pom.
2. Center the large pom-pom over four pipe cleaners.
3. Glue the pipe cleaners to the large pom-pom and let the glue dry.
4. Bend each pipe cleaner piece to make the spider's legs.
5. Glue wiggle eyes to the small pom-pom.

Direction Set B

How to Make a Spider
1. Glue two pom-poms together.
2. Glue on some pipe cleaners.
3. Bend the pipe cleaners.
4. Add eyes.

Kaylee

○ I think set A would be the best set to follow. For one thing, it tells you the exact materials you will need. Set A tells you why you need to bend the pipe cleaners. Also, set A tells you how to add the eyes.

○

Drawing Attention

Writing book titles

Materials:
10 or more books
highlighter
paper

A child chooses five books from the collection. He writes a complete sentence about each book that includes its correctly capitalized and underlined title. After he's written his sentences, he rereads each one and highlights the line under the book title.

Terrell

○ Little House in the Big Woods takes place a long
　　time ago.

I liked reading The Big Wave.

My favorite book is Charlotte's Web.

There are some very funny poems in It's Raining
　　Pigs and Noodles.

Another book by Jack Prelutsky is called
○　　Scranimals.

Handwritten Facts

Cursive

Materials:
copy of the fact list from page 96
paper

A child reads the list of facts and chooses three she likes the most. Then she writes each fact in her best cursive handwriting.

Paige

A giraffe's tongue is about
21 inches long.

Cats, rabbits, and lions can
move faster than people.

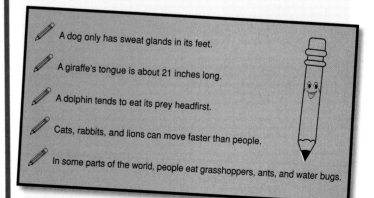

A dog only has sweat glands in its feet.

A giraffe's tongue is about 21 inches long.

A dolphin tends to eat its prey headfirst.

Cats, rabbits, and lions can move faster than people.

In some parts of the world, people eat grasshoppers, ants, and water bugs.

Sounds Like a Poem

Onomatopoeia

Materials:
word list
paper

Possible words include *buzz, hiss, zip, thump, pop, whoosh, swish, beep, click,* and *munch.*

A child folds a sheet of paper in half two times to make four sections as shown. Next, he chooses at least two words from the word list and incorporates them into a rhyming poem. He writes one line of the poem on each section of his paper. Then he draws a burst around each example of onomatopoeia and underlines his rhyming pairs.

Individual Interview

Character analysis

Materials:
cards programmed with questions like the ones shown
paper

A child writes on his paper the title of a recently read book and the author's name; then he chooses a card. He reads the card and assumes the role of one of the story's characters. He writes the character's name on his paper and then writes a response to the question from the character's point of view.

How would you describe yourself?

What is your favorite thing to do?

What is something that recently happened to you? How did you feel?

Thought Provokers

Idioms

Materials:
list of idioms like those shown
paper

A student chooses an idiom and copies it onto his paper. He reflects on a personal incident that relates to the chosen idiom and writes a brief narrative about the event. If time allows, he adds an illustration.

Idioms

Strong as an ox (really strong)

Cool as a cucumber (very calm)

Busy as a bee (very busy)

Quick as a wink (very quick)

Happy as a clam (very happy)

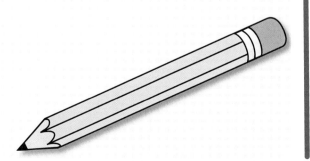

Getting to the Point

Summarizing

Materials:
student copies of page 99, cut out

After reading a book, a child writes the title in the middle of her star pattern. She writes a phrase about the story's most important events or key ideas on each of the star's rays. Then she refers to the star to write a brief paragraph summary.

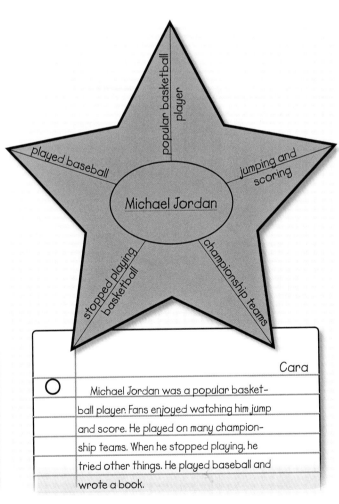

Cara

Michael Jordan was a popular basket-ball player. Fans enjoyed watching him jump and score. He played on many champion-ship teams. When he stopped playing, he tried other things. He played baseball and wrote a book.

Set 25

Pause and Separate

Commas

Materials:
student copies of page 100
scissors
glue

A child follows the directions on the reproducible to complete the activity.

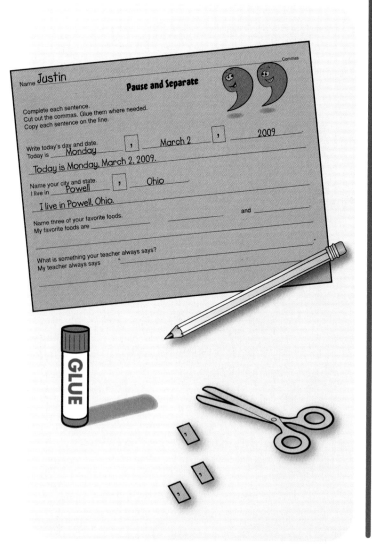

Stop, Think, Ask

Generating questions

Materials:
timer or clock
book
paper

A student folds her paper to make six sections as shown. Next, she sets the timer for a predetermined number of minutes and begins reading. When the time is up, she stops reading and writes in each section of the left column a question about upcoming events or information from her reading. The student resumes reading and then writes an answer for each question in the corresponding section of the right column. If she is unable to answer a question, she writes "n/a" in the answer section.

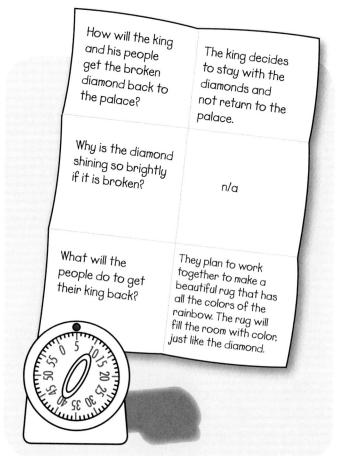

Find the Right Words

Quotation marks

Materials:
cards from page 101, cut apart
paper

A child reads each card and places it in one of two piles: correctly written or incorrectly written. When all the cards have been sorted, he writes on his paper each sentence from the incorrect pile, making the corrections needed.

Where in the World?

Atlas

Materials:
cards labeled with geographic locations, like the
    ones shown
atlas
paper

A student chooses a card and reads the location listed on it. She writes the location on her paper and then uses the atlas to find it. When she's found it, the student writes where it is, on what page it was found, and what she learned about it.

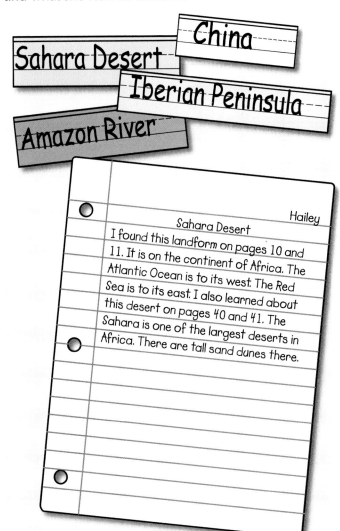

Extra Edits

Apostrophes

Materials:
student copies of the top of page 102
paper
scissors
glue

A student cuts apart the cards and places each word or phrase card on his paper. Then he places an apostrophe at the appropriate place on one card. When he's satisfied with its placement, he glues both pieces to his paper. He continues in this manner until all the cards are glued to the paper.

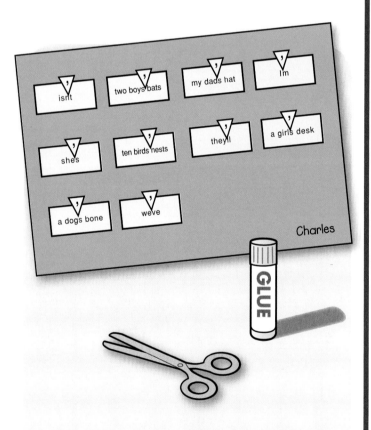

Word Pair Challenge

Homophones

Materials:
dictionary
paper

A child writes each letter of the alphabet on her paper and writes a homophone pair for as many letters as possible. If needed, she refers to a dictionary to confirm her pairing or to check her spelling.

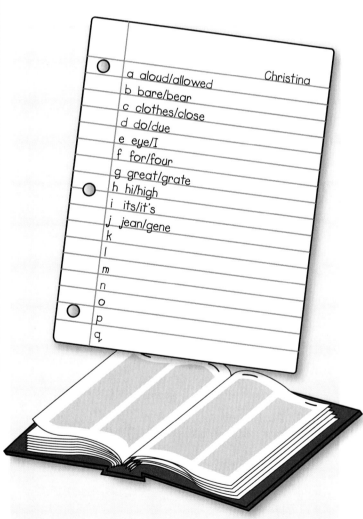

Mix 'n' Match Story

Imaginative narrative

Materials:
fiction books or stories that students have previously read
paper

A child chooses a character from one story, a setting from another story, and a problem from a third story. He organizes each story element in a web on his paper and then generates a solution of his own. Then he combines the story elements to write an imaginative narrative.

Rhyme Time

Poetry

Materials:
student copies of the poetry frame on the bottom
　of page 102
paper

A child chooses a topic, writes it on her paper, and writes a related term in each box. Next, she generates a list of rhyming words for each term. She refers to the words to write a poem on the lines provided. If desired, she copies her poem onto another sheet of paper.

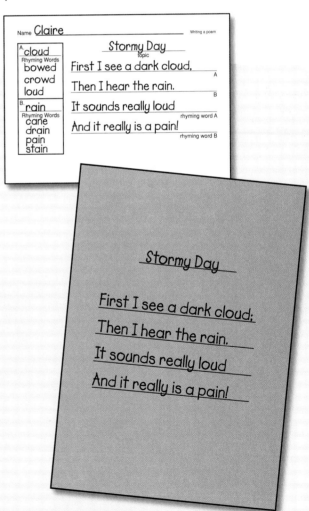

Feelings All Around

Words to express mood

Materials:
circle template
paper
scissors

A child traces the circle template on his paper and then cuts it out. Next, he folds the circle in half two times and then unfolds it to make four equal sections. He labels each section with a word that describes a mood. Then he lists in each section words and phrases that help create a mental picture of the mood. The student refers to the lists at a later date to help express the tone of his writing.

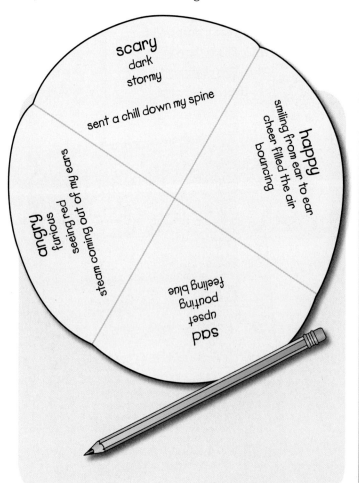

Topping It Off

Prefixes

Materials:
2 cards labeled with prefixes
cards labeled with base words, cut slightly shorter than the
    prefix cards
dictionary
paper

A student folds her paper in half, unfolds it, and labels each resulting column with a prefix. Next, she places a base word card atop each prefix card, in turn. She writes the combination that makes a real word in the corresponding column. If neither combination results in a word, the student moves the base word card to a discard pile. When all the words have been recorded, she uses the dictionary to check her work.

Side by Side

Characters

Materials:
recently read book
paper
ruler

A student uses the ruler to make a chart with three columns and five rows on his paper. He labels the top row with the title of a recently read book and two of the story's characters. Then he labels each row in the left column as shown. He completes each section of the chart, referring to the book as needed.

Keeping It Straight

Paragraphs

Materials:
4 cards labeled with sequence words
index cards (four per student)
paper

A child plans the main events of her story or main points of her report, writing each idea on an index card. Next, she orders the sequence cards on her workspace and places each of her idea cards under its corresponding sequence card. Then she refers to the cards as she writes her draft, adding details where needed.

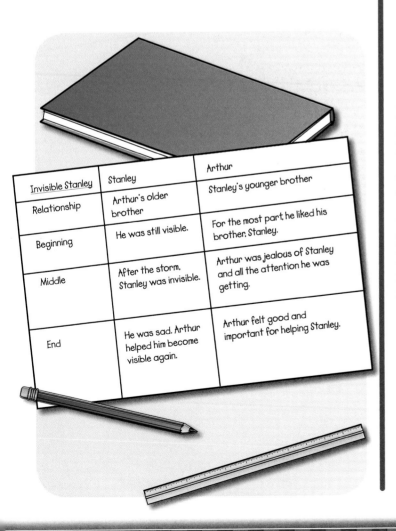

Invisible Stanley	Stanley	Arthur
Relationship	Arthur's older brother	Stanley's younger brother
Beginning	He was still visible.	For the most part, he liked his brother, Stanley.
Middle	After the storm, Stanley was invisible.	Arthur was jealous of Stanley and all the attention he was getting.
End	He was sad. Arthur helped him become visible again.	Arthur felt good and important for helping Stanley.

First

new moon, can't see light

After that

first quarter, actually see half moon

Later

full moon, see fully lit moon

Finally

end of cycle, last quarter, half moon again

Mia

During each month, we see the different phases of the moon. First, we see the new moon. That means we can't see any light reflecting off the moon. The new moon phase actually shows us no moon at all. After that, we see the first quarter moon. At this phase, we see half of the moon. Later in the cycle, we see a full moon. Finally, at the end of the cycle, we see a half moon again. This time it is the last quarter. Even though we see changes in the moon from phase to phase, these are the four main phases we see.

Put In Place

Common forms of literature

Materials:
student copies of the sorting cards on page 103
paper
scissors
glue

A student folds a sheet of paper into four equal sections and labels each section as shown. Next, he looks at the cards in the left column of his copy and writes on the cards an example of each form of literature. He cuts apart these cards and glues each in its corresponding section. Then he cuts apart the remaining cards, determines in which section each card should be placed, and glues the cards to his paper.

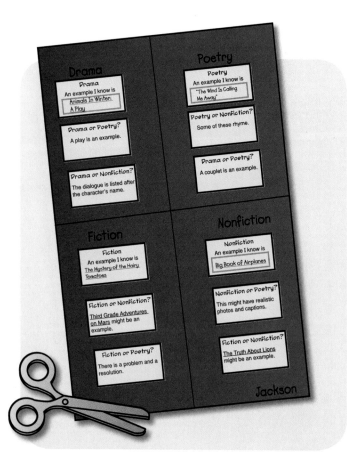

Words to Investigate

Using an index

Materials:
copy of the question cards on the bottom of page 103 programmed to correspond with a textbook, cut apart and placed in a bag
textbook
paper

A child selects a question card and writes the corresponding number on her paper. She uses the textbook's index to find the answer and writes the answer on her paper. The child continues in this manner until she has answered a predetermined number of questions. Then she returns the questions to the bag.

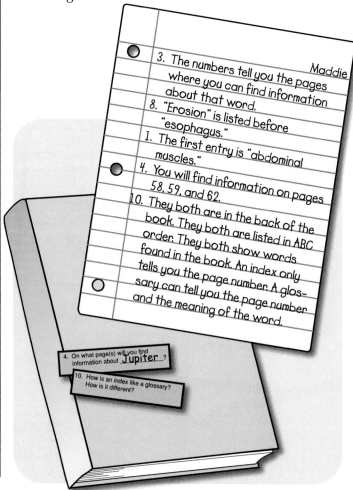

Just Saying

Quotation marks

Materials:
magazines and calendars with animal pictures
paper
scissors
glue

A student selects an animal picture, cuts it out, and glues it to his paper. He writes near the animal's head a statement the animal might say and then draws a speech bubble around the statement. After that, the child writes the animal's statement in a direct quotation.

More and More

Elaboration

Materials:
paper
scissors

A child folds a sheet of paper in half two times and then unfolds it. She cuts a diagonal line up from each bottom corner to make a triangle. In the top section, she writes the name of a character in a story she's about to write. In each remaining section, she writes more information about the character and how the character will be involved in her story. She uses the resulting organizer to help her write a well-elaborated story at another time.

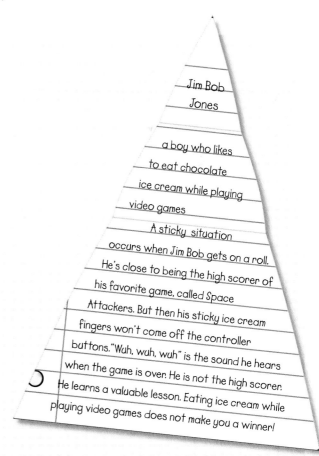

Set 29

Covered Up

Abbreviations

Materials:
student copies of the grid on page 104
copy of the cards on page 104, cut apart
paper

A child writes a different word from the word bank in each section of the grid. Then he chooses a card, identifies the abbreviation, and places it on the corresponding section. When the student has completed his grid, he writes each word and its abbreviation on his paper.

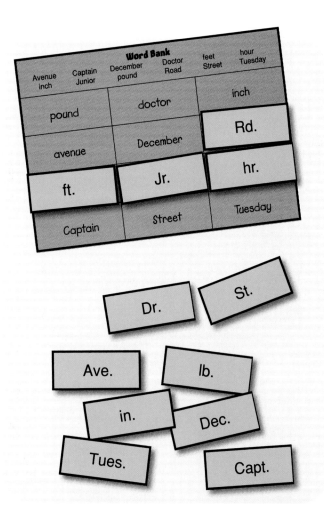

Flagged

Referencing text to support answers

Materials:
reading selection with questions
sticky notes (one per question per child)
paper

A student reviews the reading selection's questions. Then she writes the question number and a key phrase from each question on a sticky note. When she comes across information in her reading that leads her to an answer, she places the corresponding sticky note on that page. When she is ready to write answers to the questions, she refers back to the marked pages, citing evidence from those pages in her response.

When and Where

Setting

Materials:
paper
highlighter

A child divides his paper into nine sections, writes the titles of two recently read stories across the top, and labels two side sections as shown. He writes details about each book's setting in the corresponding sections and then highlights similarities between the two books. At a later time, the student refers to the chart to write about how the settings are alike and how they're different.

	Yeh-Shen	Domitila: A Cinderella Tale From the Mexican Tradition
Where?	southern China stepmother's home pond	rancho in Hidalgo, Mexico the grand mansion of the governor her father and stepmother's home
When?	in the dim past over time festival time	over time Hidalgo Fall Festival

Recording Some Laughs

Cursive

Materials:
joke and riddle books
index cards (one per child)

A child reviews the books and locates a joke or riddle she enjoys. Then she uses her best cursive writing to record the setup on one side of a card and the punch line on the other.

Why do bees have sticky hair?

They use honey combs.

What's full of holes but still holds water?

How much is a skunk worth?

Solving the Puzzles

Problem and solution

Materials:
books (two per child)
student copies of page 105
12" x 18" paper (one sheet per child)
scissors
glue

A student cuts out the puzzle pieces, puts the matching pieces together, and writes the problem and solution for each of two stories on the corresponding pieces. She glues the puzzle pieces to her paper; then she refers to the resulting organizer as she writes at the bottom of her paper to compare and contrast the story elements.

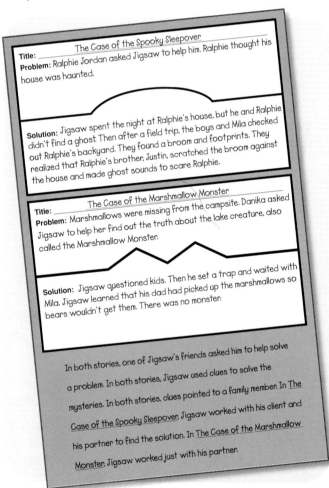

Title: _The Case of the Spooky Sleepover_
Problem: Ralphie Jordan asked Jigsaw to help him. Ralphie thought his house was haunted.

Solution: Jigsaw spent the night at Ralphie's house, but he and Ralphie didn't find a ghost. Then after a field trip, the boys and Mila checked out Ralphie's backyard. They found a broom and footprints. They realized that Ralphie's brother, Justin, scratched the broom against the house and made ghost sounds to scare Ralphie.

Title: _The Case of the Marshmallow Monster_
Problem: Marshmallows were missing from the campsite. Danika asked Jigsaw to help her find out the truth about the lake creature, also called the Marshmallow Monster.

Solution: Jigsaw questioned kids. Then he set a trap and waited with Mila. Jigsaw learned that his dad had picked up the marshmallows so bears wouldn't get them. There was no monster.

In both stories, one of Jigsaw's friends asked him to help solve a problem. In both stories, Jigsaw used clues to solve the mysteries. In both stories, clues pointed to a family member. In _The Case of the Spooky Sleepover_, Jigsaw worked with his client and his partner to find the solution. In _The Case of the Marshmallow Monster_, Jigsaw worked just with his partner.

Fitting In

Guide words

Materials:
tagboard copy of page 106 assembled as directed
paper

A child writes the guide words from the mat on his paper. Then he gently pulls the strip to reveal each word. He writes on his paper each word that could be on a dictionary page with the named guide words.

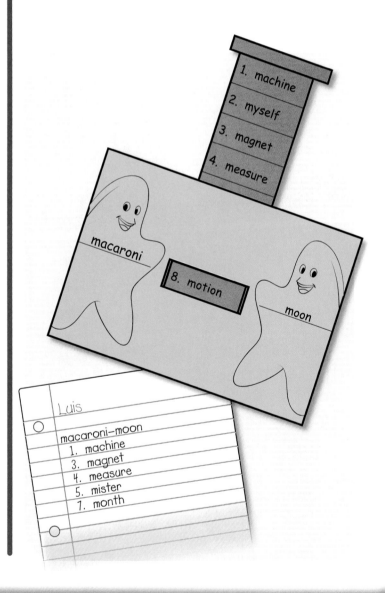

1. machine
2. myself
3. magnet
4. measure

macaroni

8. motion

moon

Luis

macaroni–moon
1. machine
3. magnet
4. measure
5. mister
7. month

How Do They Stack Up?

Story elements

Materials:
paper (three sheets per child)
stapler
scissors

A student stacks three sheets of paper and then staggers them as shown. He folds the stack to create six flaps and staples the resulting booklet along the fold. Next, he cuts a vertical slit in the middle of the top five flaps, leaving the bottom page intact. He labels each flap at the top of the booklet with a different book title and author. Then he labels each row of remaining flaps with a different story element. Finally, he lifts each flap and writes information about the corresponding story element.

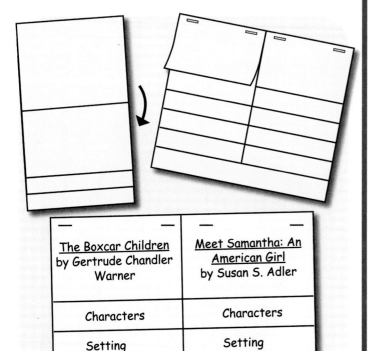

The Boxcar Children by Gertrude Chandler Warner	Meet Samantha: An American Girl by Susan S. Adler
Characters	Characters
Setting	Setting
Problem	Problem
Solution	Solution
Theme	Theme

Published Pages

Report writing

Materials:
student copies of page 107

After researching a chosen topic, a child titles her paper as though it is part of a children's magazine. She writes her main report on the lines and writes an interesting fact in the burst. Then, in the box, she draws a picture related to her topic and adds a caption below.

Living the Life of a Butterfly

by Nicole

A butterfly goes through four stages of development. This is called metamorphosis. First, an adult butterfly lays an egg. The egg is usually laid on a plant. After some time, the egg hatches. A caterpillar comes from the egg. The caterpillar eats and eats. It also sheds its skin. Then it forms a shell known as a chrysalis. The caterpillar is growing into a butterfly inside this shell. When it is ready, the adult butterfly comes out.

A butterfly uses its sight and smell to find a mate.

Most caterpillars eat green plants.

Figurative Phrases

Idioms

Materials:
copy of page 108, cut and folded to create tents
paper

A child copies on the left side of her paper an idiom from a tent and illustrates its literal meaning. Then she writes on the right side of her paper the meaning of the phrase, referring to the opposite side of the tent for clarification if needed. She repeats the process on the back of her paper with a different idiom.

a pretty penny

a lot of money

a pretty penny

My mom said that her new car cost a pretty penny. My dad was not happy that she spent a lot of money on it.

Partners in Rhyme

Poetry

Materials:
poetry books
paper

A child locates a rhyming poem in one of the books. She writes on her paper the book's title, the poem's title, and the page number. Next, the student writes the poem's rhyme scheme and the words from a rhyming pair in the poem. Then she lists other words that match the rhyming pair.

Elise

The New Kid on the Block
"My Baby Brother"
page 61
aabab
b = week, leak
beak, creak, meek, peak, seek, sleek

The New Kid on the Block

Jack Prelutsky

Stellar Work

Proofreading for spelling

For partners

Materials:
dictionary
pen
paper

A child completes an assigned writing activity and then exchanges papers with a partner. The partner proofreads her writing, using a pen to circle any words he feels might be misspelled. He returns the paper to the owner, who checks the dictionary to confirm her spellings. If she spelled a circled word correctly, she draws a star above it. If she misspelled the word, she erases the word and then writes it correctly in the circle.

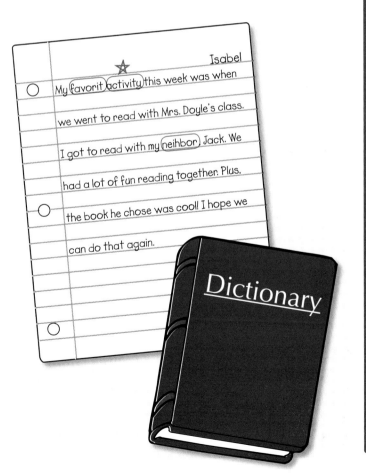

Isabel

My favorit activity this week was when

we went to read with Mrs. Doyle's class.

I got to read with my neihbor Jack. We

had a lot of fun reading together. Plus,

the book he chose was cool! I hope we

can do that again.

Dictionary

Draw the Line

Capitalization

Materials:
copy of a numbered passage with capitalization errors, placed in a plastic sheet protector
wipe-off marker
paper towel
paper

A student reads the passage and underlines any capitalization errors. When he's satisfied with his work, he writes on his paper the line number of each mistake, writes the word correctly, and tells why the word should be capitalized. Then he wipes his page protector clean.

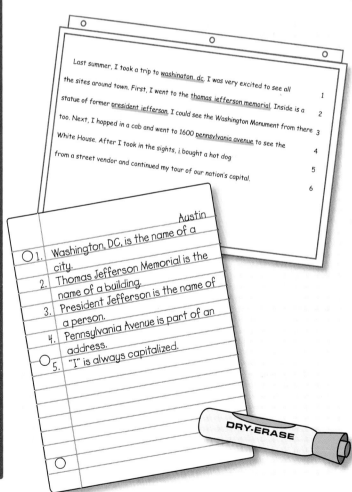

Last summer, I took a trip to washinaton, dc. I was very excited to see all the sites around town. First, I went to the thomas jefferson memorial. Inside is a statue of former president jefferson. I could see the Washington Monument from there too. Next, I hopped in a cab and went to 1600 pennsylvania avenue to see the White House. After I took in the sights, i bought a hot dog from a street vendor and continued my tour of our nation's capital.

1
2
3
4
5
6

Austin

1. Washington, DC, is the name of a city.
2. Thomas Jefferson Memorial is the name of a building.
3. President Jefferson is the name of a person.
4. Pennsylvania Avenue is part of an address.
5. "I" is always capitalized.

DRY-ERASE

The Short Version

Summarizing

Materials:
recently read book
index cards (one per child)

After reading, a child reflects on what she's read. For a fiction text, she considers who the story is mostly about, what the problem is, and how the problem is solved. For nonfiction texts, she determines the main topic and the most important facts. Then she challenges herself to write the information in three sentences or less.

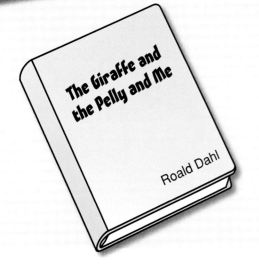

The Giraffe and the Pelly and Me
① The giraffe, monkey, and pelican spent all their money to open a window-cleaning company and were too poor to buy food. ② They were hired to wash the Duke of Hampshire's 677 windows and, while there, helped him catch a thief. ③ The Duke was so thankful, he offered to take care of the animals for the rest of their lives.

The Giraffe and
the Pelly and Me

Roald Dahl

Reference Q & A

Dictionary

For partners

Materials:
student dictionaries (one per child)
list of words, like the one shown
paper

Each student chooses a word from the list and locates it in a dictionary. They each write a question based on the word's entries and then exchange papers. Each partner then uses the dictionary to answer the question, noting the page on which the answer was found. The students continue in this manner as time allows.

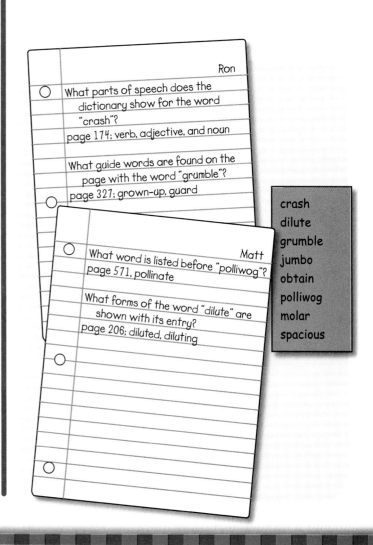

Ron

○ What parts of speech does the dictionary show for the word "crash"?
page 174; verb, adjective, and noun

What guide words are found on the page with the word "grumble"?
page 327; grown-up, guard

Matt

○ What word is listed before "polliwog"?
page 571; pollinate

What forms of the word "dilute" are shown with its entry?
page 206; diluted, diluting

crash
dilute
grumble
jumbo
obtain
polliwog
molar
spacious

Squared Away

Homophones

Materials:
square sheets of paper (one per child)
homophone word list, like the one shown

A student folds his paper in half two times and unfolds it to reveal four square sections. Then the student folds each corner toward the center to make four flaps. The child writes a word from the list on a flap and then writes a sentence using the word. He flips the flap up, writes the corresponding homophone, and writes a sentence using that word. He continues in this manner, using a different homophone pair on each flap.

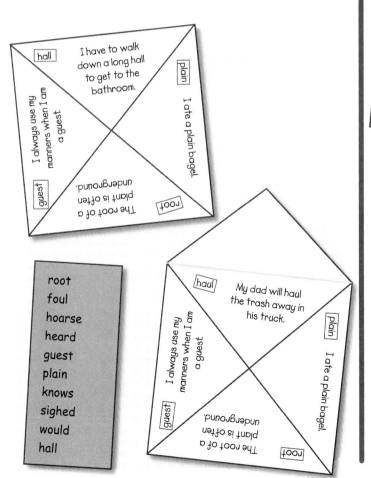

root
foul
hoarse
heard
guest
plain
knows
sighed
would
hall

Pick a Play

Writing dramas

Materials:
cards labeled with quick classroom activities, like the ones shown
cards labeled with student names
paper

A child chooses an activity card and writes information about the scene at the top of her paper. Then she chooses two cards with student names to serve as the characters and writes dialogue to match the event.

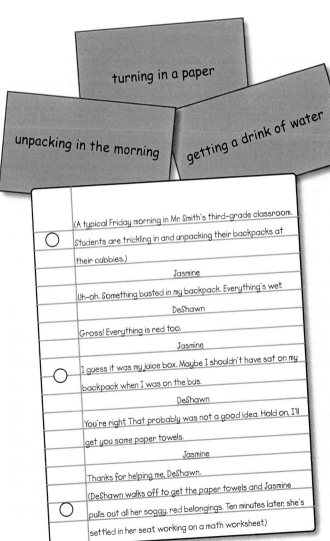

Check This Out

Reference skills

Materials:
chapter book
paper

Before reading a chapter book, a student divides her paper into two columns and labels the columns with the questions shown. She refers to the chapter titles in the table of contents to determine what story information she can assume and what questions can be asked about the story. Then, at another time, she reads the book to confirm or reject her statements, silently answering the questions as she reads.

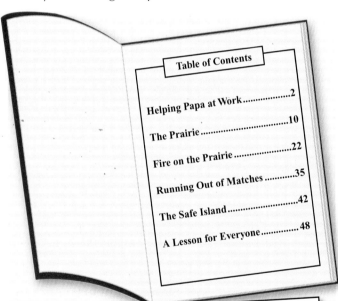

Table of Contents

Helping Papa at Work 2

The Prairie 10

Fire on the Prairie 22

Running Out of Matches 35

The Safe Island 42

A Lesson for Everyone 48

What Do I Know?
The story takes place on a prairie.

There's a fire on the prairie.

What Can I Ask?
What is Papa's job?

How did the fire start?

Why are matches being lit after the fire starts?

How can there be an island on a prairie?

Erik

The Big Top

Main idea and details

Materials:
reading selection
crayons or colored pencils
paper

A child draws on her paper a circus tent like the one shown. She writes the main idea of her reading selection on the tent's top and the supporting details along the sides of the tent.

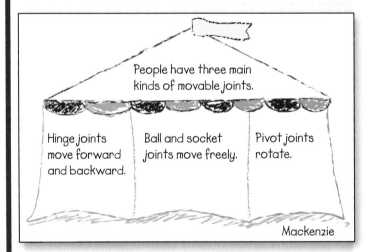

People have three main kinds of movable joints.

Hinge joints move forward and backward.

Ball and socket joints move freely.

Pivot joints rotate.

Mackenzie

In Training

Text connections

Materials:
student copies of the dumbbell pattern on page 109
scissors

A child writes on the left side of the dumbbell pattern information about a recently read story that leads him to a connection. Next, he writes on the right side information about another book, personal experience, or world event and explains the connection between the two. Then he cuts out the pattern.

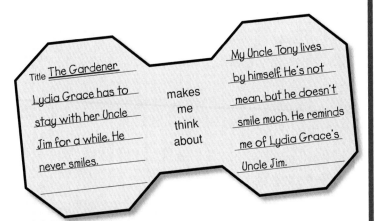

Title The Gardener
Lydia Grace has to stay with her Uncle Jim for a while. He never smiles.

makes me think about

My Uncle Tony lives by himself. He's not mean, but he doesn't smile much. He reminds me of Lydia Grace's Uncle Jim.

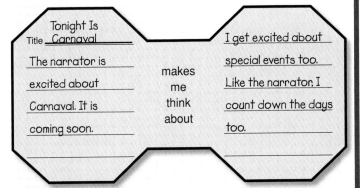

Title Tonight Is Carnaval
The narrator is excited about Carnaval. It is coming soon.

makes me think about

I get excited about special events too. Like the narrator, I count down the days too.

Picturing the Past

Personal narrative

Materials:
paper
crayons

A child reflects on a favorite memory from the school year and then draws and labels in the middle of her paper a simple picture that represents that memory. She writes details associated with the event around the picture. The student uses her plan to write a personal narrative.

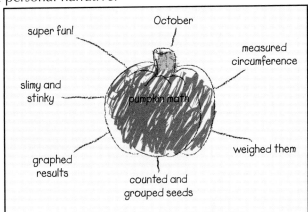

super fun! October
measured circumference
slimy and stinky
pumpkin math
graphed results
counted and grouped seeds
weighed them

Michelle

I will never forget the fun we had with pumpkin math at the end of October. When we came in that day, we noticed that there were several pumpkins on the back table. There were also some parents walking around the room. We had to wait through morning announcements before Ms. Pastino gave us the good news. We were going to spend the morning doing math with the pumpkins.

Each table was given a pumpkin. First, we measured around our pumpkin's middle. We learned that this is called the circumference. Then we weighed our pumpkin. After that, Matt's mom helped us cut open our pumpkin. We reached in and pulled out the slimy seeds. The room got stinky really fast. But it was still fun. We counted and grouped our seeds. Then we shared each group's data and made a graph for the task. By the time we had finished our work and cleaned up, it was time for lunch. The morning just flew by.

Keys to Pronunciation

Dictionary

Materials:
copies of the key patterns on page 109 (one per child)
list of words like the one shown
dictionary
paper
scissors
glue

A child cuts out two keys, labels each key with a different skill from the word list, and glues the keys to the top of her paper. Next, the student checks the dictionary to confirm the pronunciation of each word on the list. When she has found the pronunciation, she writes the word under the corresponding key and records the page number.

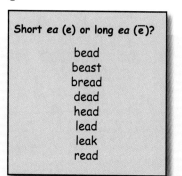

Short *ea* (e) or long *ea* (ē)?

bead
beast
bread
dead
head
lead
leak
read

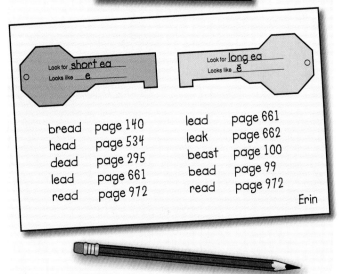

Look for short ea
Looks like e

Look for long ea
Looks like ē

bread	page 140	lead	page 661
head	page 534	leak	page 662
dead	page 295	beast	page 100
lead	page 661	bead	page 99
read	page 972	read	page 972

Erin

ABCs of Opposites

Antonyms

Materials:
letter cards in a paper bag
paper

A student selects a card from the bag and writes the letter on his paper. He records as many antonym pairs as he can name, with at least one word in each pair starting with the selected letter. When he is satisfied with his list, he returns the card to the bag and selects another one.

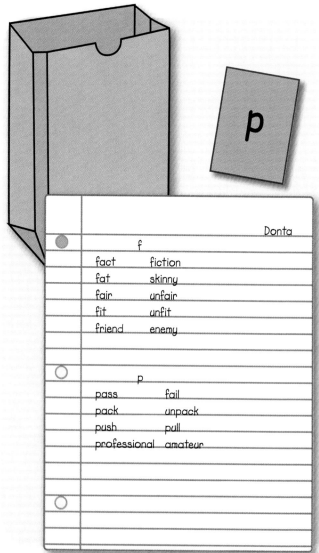

Donta

f

fact	fiction
fat	skinny
fair	unfair
fit	unfit
friend	enemy

p

pass	fail
pack	unpack
push	pull
professional	amateur

Pocket-Size Poems

Poetry

Materials:
poetry frame like the one shown
magazines and newspapers
blank cards (one per child)
scissors
glue

A student chooses an interesting picture that will fit on his card and cuts it out. He refers to his picture and the poetry frame to write a poem on his card. Then he turns the card over and glues his picture to the back.

Cinquain Poetry Frame
Line 1: Name for the picture
Line 2: Adjective, adjective
Line 3: -ing verb, -ing verb, -ing verb
Line 4: Four-word phrase with a verb
Line 5: Synonym for line 1

Chimpanzees
Supportive, watchful
Standing, caring, exploring
Checking out their habitat
Primates

Hidden Meaning

Author's theme

Materials:
construction paper (one sheet per child)
blank paper
stapler
scissors
crayons or colored pencils

A child places her construction paper atop the blank paper and staples it in place. Next, she cuts the construction paper to look like stage curtains. She draws on the blank paper a scene from a recently read story and writes a brief summary of the story under the illustration. The student then lifts the curtains to write the author's theme.

In *The Little Red Hen*, the hen worked hard to prepare a loaf of bread from scratch. She asked the other animals to help, but they would not. When it was time to eat the bread, all the animals wanted some. The hen wouldn't let the animals have any.

In this story, the author wants to show that being lazy will get you nothing in return.

In *The Little Red Hen*, the hen worked hard to prepare a loaf of bread from scratch. She asked the other animals to help, but they would not. When it was time to eat the bread, all the animals wanted some. The hen wouldn't let the animals have any.

Customized Clues

Common forms of literature

Materials:
index cards (four per child)
hole puncher
metal ring

A child writes clues about a form of literature on the front of a card and the answer on the back. She completes three more cards in this manner, with each card describing and naming a different form of literature. The student hole-punches the same corner of each card and binds the cards together with a metal ring.

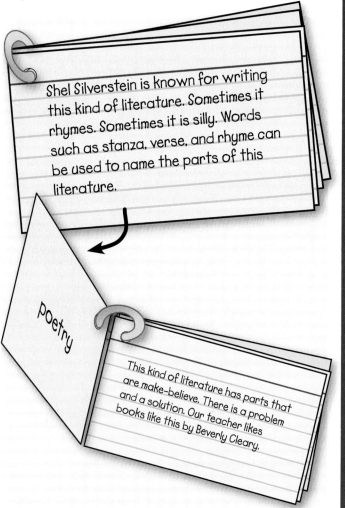

Shel Silverstein is known for writing this kind of literature. Sometimes it rhymes. Sometimes it is silly. Words such as stanza, verse, and rhyme can be used to name the parts of this literature.

poetry

This kind of literature has parts that are make-believe. There is a problem and a solution. Our teacher likes books like this by Beverly Cleary.

Wheels in Motion

Plural nouns

Materials:
copy of the wheel patterns on page 110, cut apart and assembled as shown
paper

A child divides his paper into six sections and numbers each section as shown. He turns the wheel to the first section, reads the direction, and writes a word on his paper that matches the direction. Then he moves the wheel to the next section and repeats the process. The child continues in this manner as time allows.

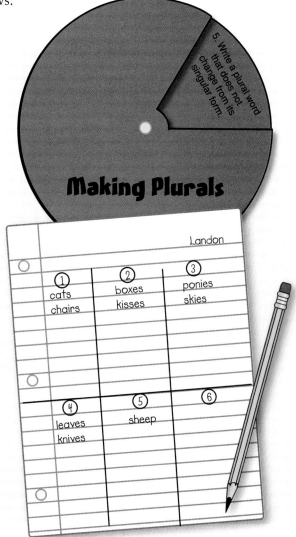

5. Write a plural word that does not change from its singular form.

Making Plurals

Landon

①	②	③
cats	boxes	ponies
chairs	kisses	skies

④	⑤	⑥
leaves	sheep	
knives		

Rounding Up Words

Suffixes

Materials:
cards labeled with root words
card labeled with suffixes
paper

Possible base words include *beauty, break, color, comfort, delight, enjoy, home, hug, love, play, power,* and *wire.*

A child draws three circles on his paper and then writes a different suffix and its meaning in each. Next, he chooses a base word card and determines which of the three suffixes, if any, he can add to the root word to make a word. Then he writes each resulting word in the corresponding circle. He continues in this manner as time allows.

-ful (full of)
-less (not having)
-able (capable of)

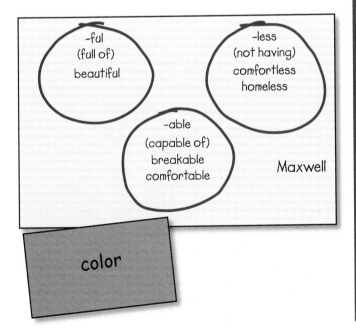

Time to Reflect

Letter writing

Materials:
paper

A student reflects on a kind act someone did for her or one that she witnessed in the recent past. She writes a letter about the event to the person who did the kind act, using proper friendly letter form.

May 19, 2009

Dear Katie,
   How are you? I hope that you are doing well. I am writing to thank you for sharing your snack with me last week. I can't believe I left mine at home that day. I never do that! I was pretty sad about it. You were nice enough to share your pretzels with me. That made me feel a lot better. Thanks for being a nice classmate.

Your friend,
Keshia

Timely Tips

Expository writing

Materials:
envelopes (one per child)
paper

A child reflects on something he has learned and writes the topic on an envelope. Then he writes on his paper at least one paragraph, describing to another student the steps to complete the task. If time allows, the child tests his directions to make sure they are complete and accurate before he tucks his writing inside his envelope.

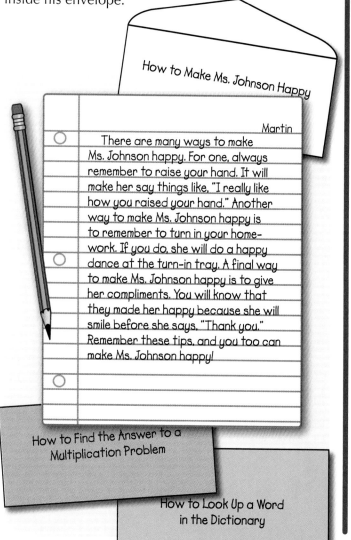

A Guiding Star

Nonfiction text features

Materials:
tagboard star template, labeled with questions like the ones shown
textbook
paper

A student traces the star onto his paper. Then he locates a graph, chart, or diagram in his textbook. He writes above his tracing the page where he found the text feature. Then he reads each question on the star template and writes each answer in a section of his star.

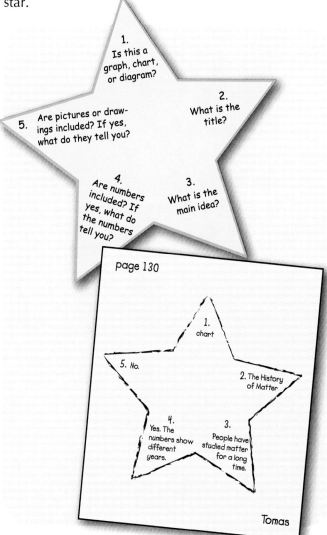

Clip and Sort

Compound words

Materials:
magazines and newspapers
paper
scissors
pen
glue

A child folds his paper in half, unfolds it, and labels each section as shown. Then he searches magazines or newspapers for examples of compound words. When he finds one, he cuts it out, underlines both of the smaller words in the compound word, and glues the cutout in the corresponding column.

What Do You Know?

Punctuation

Materials:
list of questions like the ones shown
5½" x 8½" paper strips (two per child)
stapler

A child stacks and folds her paper strips to make a booklet and staples the booklet along the fold. She writes a question from the list on the top page and uses her knowledge of punctuation rules to write the answer and examples on the back. The student alternates questions and answers in this manner until she has written all four.

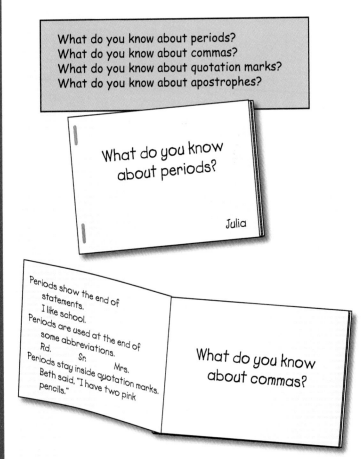

High-Frequency Word Cards and Gameboard
Use with "Covered!" on page 4.

about <small>TEC61150</small>	because <small>TEC61150</small>	could <small>TEC61150</small>	during <small>TEC61150</small>	every <small>TEC61150</small>	friend <small>TEC61150</small>
guess <small>TEC61150</small>	idea <small>TEC61150</small>	just <small>TEC61150</small>	know <small>TEC61150</small>	laugh <small>TEC61150</small>	often <small>TEC61150</small>
our <small>TEC61150</small>	people <small>TEC61150</small>	read <small>TEC61150</small>	receive <small>TEC61150</small>	said <small>TEC61150</small>	shown <small>TEC61150</small>
special <small>TEC61150</small>	their <small>TEC61150</small>	there <small>TEC61150</small>	thought <small>TEC61150</small>	until <small>TEC61150</small>	used <small>TEC61150</small>

Covered!

					TEC61150

Super Simple Independent Practice: Language Arts • ©The Mailbox® Books • TEC61150

Name _____

Name That Page

Use two different textbooks to complete the charts.

Title of book:	Title of book:
How many chapters are there?	How many chapters are there?
On what page does chapter 4 begin?	On what page does chapter 4 begin?
In which chapter would you find page 22?	In which chapter would you find page 22?
Does the book have a glossary? If so, write the glossary's first word.	Does the book have a glossary? If so, write the glossary's first word.
On what page does the index begin?	On what page does the index begin?
Which chapter is the longest?	Which chapter is the longest?
Which chapter is the shortest?	Which chapter is the shortest?
Which chapter title interests you the most?	Which chapter title interests you the most?

Super Simple Independent Practice: Language Arts • ©The Mailbox® Books • TEC61150

Note to the teacher: Use with "Name That Page" on page 7.

77

Cloud and Raindrop Patterns

Use with "Raindrop Race" on page 8.

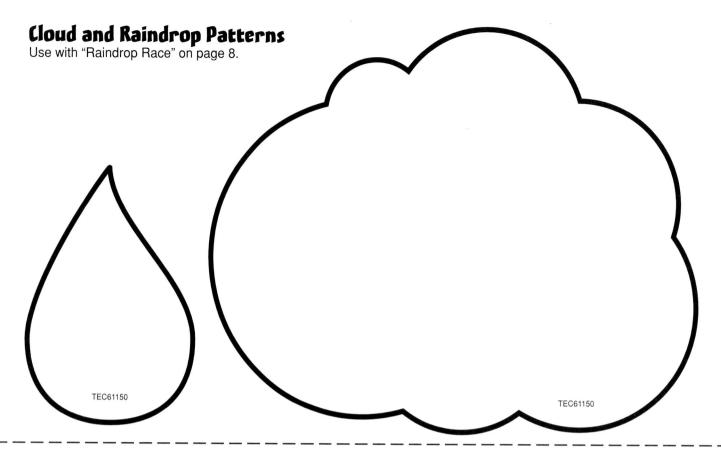

TEC61150

TEC61150

Name _____ Capitalization

Capitalize the World

A	B	C
D	E	F
G	H	I
J	K	L
M	N	O
P	Q	R
S	T	U
V	W	X
Y	Z	

Note to the teacher: Use with "Places to Go" on page 9.

In Gear for Antonyms

_____ / _____   _____ / _____

_____ / _____   _____ / _____

_____ / _____   _____ / _____

_____ / _____   _____ / _____

_____ / _____   _____ / _____

_____ / _____   _____ / _____

_____ / _____   _____ / _____

_____ / _____   _____ / _____

Super Simple Independent Practice: Language Arts • ©The Mailbox® Books • TEC61150

Note to the teacher: Use with "Left Foot, Right Foot" on page 10.

79

Word Cards

Use with "Red-Letter Words" on page 12.

speed TEC61150	dream	queen
teach	greet	please
teeth	peach	creek
wheat	wheel	bean
cheer	steam	three
bead	sleep	flea

Sentence Cards

Use with "Sentence or Not?" on page 13.

Soccer ball missing. TEC61150	Bob's new soccer ball is missing. TEC61150
First, he in his room. TEC61150	First, he searched in his room. TEC61150
He in the hall closet. TEC61150	Next, he looked in the hall closet. TEC61150
Finally, he to the basement. TEC61150	Finally, he went down to the basement. TEC61150
That where found new soccer ball. TEC61150	That is where he found his new soccer ball. TEC61150

Super Simple Independent Practice: Language Arts • ©The Mailbox® Books • TEC61150

It rained today. TEC61150	Laura Ingalls Wilder TEC61150	*The Ugly Duckling* TEC61150
Fourth of July TEC61150	Wednesday TEC61150	Chicago, Illinois TEC61150
Grand Canyon TEC61150	They left yesterday. TEC61150	Rosa Parks TEC61150
"The Star-Spangled Banner" TEC61150	Thanksgiving TEC61150	Washington, DC TEC61150
Sunday TEC61150	Statue of Liberty TEC61150	*The Three Little Pigs* TEC61150
The little dog ran. TEC61150	George Washington TEC61150	January TEC61150
Memorial Day TEC61150	Florida TEC61150	Golden Gate Bridge TEC61150
August TEC61150	Jackie Robinson TEC61150	*Charlotte's Web* TEC61150

Pear Patterns

Use with "Quite a Pair!" on page 16.

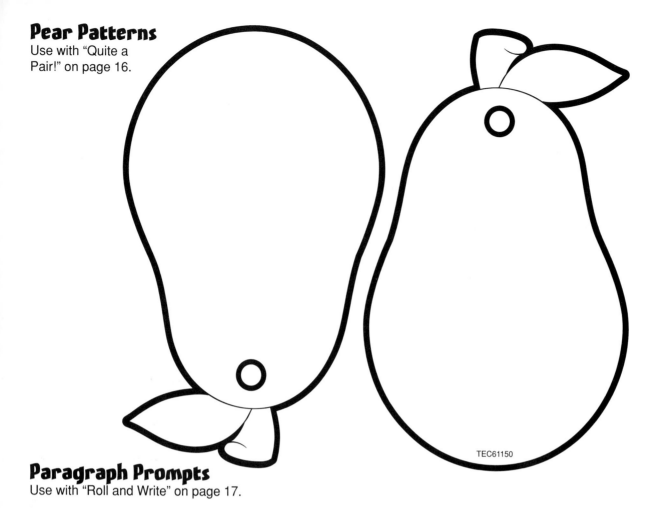

TEC61150

Paragraph Prompts

Use with "Roll and Write" on page 17.

Roll and Write

Topic Sentence	Closing Sentence
1. I'll never forget my special birthday.	It was one of my best birthdays.
2. The rain spoiled our plans.	Rainy days can be disappointing.
3. My best friend was upset with me.	I'm glad we worked things out.
4. I'll never forget the time I won something.	Winning is so much fun!
5. Taking care of a pet is hard work.	A pet is a big commitment.
6. My family and I like helping each other.	My family is very helpful.

TEC61150

b ___ b __ t TEC61150	c __ st cr __ TEC61150
fl __ fl __ t TEC61150	g __ t gr __ n TEC61150
l __ d l __ n TEC61150	m __ m __ n TEC61150
b __ l bl __ TEC61150	thr __ thr __ t TEC61150
t __ st t __ TEC61150	cr __ k c __ l TEC61150
r __ r __ st TEC61150	sn __ s __ p TEC61150

Lunchbox Pattern
Use with "What's for Lunch?" on page 19.

_____'s Lunchbox

TEC61150

Picture Cards

Use with "Add -s or -es" on page 20.

desk TEC61150	tack TEC61150	eraser TEC61150	dress TEC61150
chair TEC61150	pencil TEC61150	paintbrush TEC61150	lunchbox TEC61150
watch TEC61150	crayon TEC61150	puzzle TEC61150	backpack TEC61150

Wheel Pattern

Use with "'Wheel-ly' Cool Nouns" on page 21.

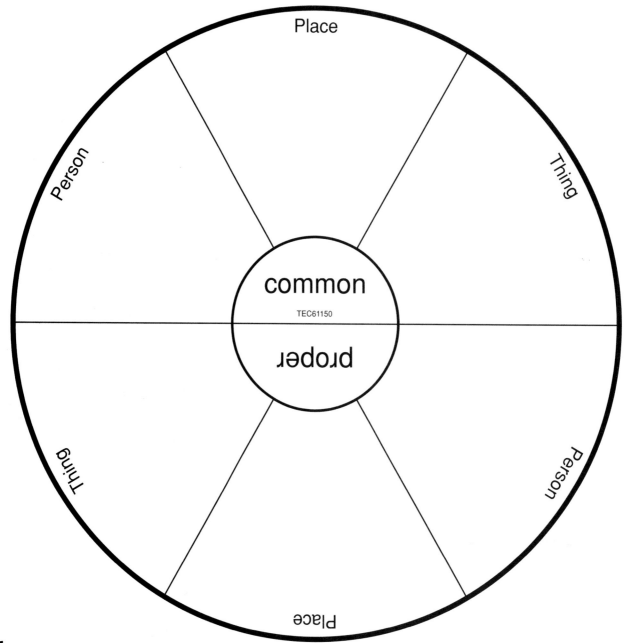

Super Simple Independent Practice: Language Arts • ©The Mailbox® Books • TEC61150

TEC61150

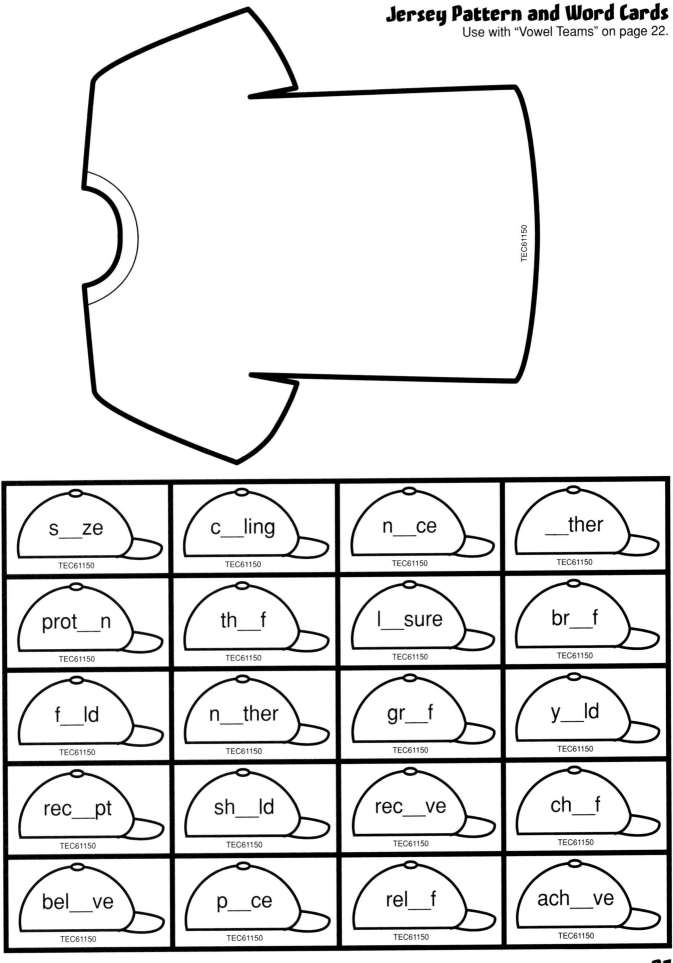

s__ze	c__ling	n__ce	__ther
prot__n	th__f	l__sure	br__f
f__ld	n__ther	gr__f	y__ld
rec__pt	sh__ld	rec__ve	ch__f
bel__ve	p__ce	rel__f	ach__ve

TEC61150 (on each card)

Possessive Noun Cards

Use with "Apostrophe Alert" on page 24.

dogs' owners TEC61150	boss's meeting TEC61150
trees' leaves TEC61150	James's mother TEC61150
students' books TEC61150	girls' bicycles TEC61150
Carlos's cat TEC61150	states' capitals TEC61150
ladies' shoes TEC61150	farmers' cows TEC61150
birds' nests TEC61150	dress's button TEC61150
class's teacher TEC61150	sneakers' laces TEC61150
Chris's homework TEC61150	sisters' dolls TEC61150
foxes' tails TEC61150	witness's story TEC61150
coaches' teams TEC61150	waitress's apron TEC61150
walrus's tusk TEC61150	bus's tire TEC61150
guests' towels TEC61150	grass's roots TEC61150

Super Simple Independent Practice: Language Arts • ©The Mailbox® Books • TEC61150

Cube Pattern

Use with "It's a Toss-Up" on page 26,
"Make the Connection" on page 38, and
"Back of the Book" on page 41.

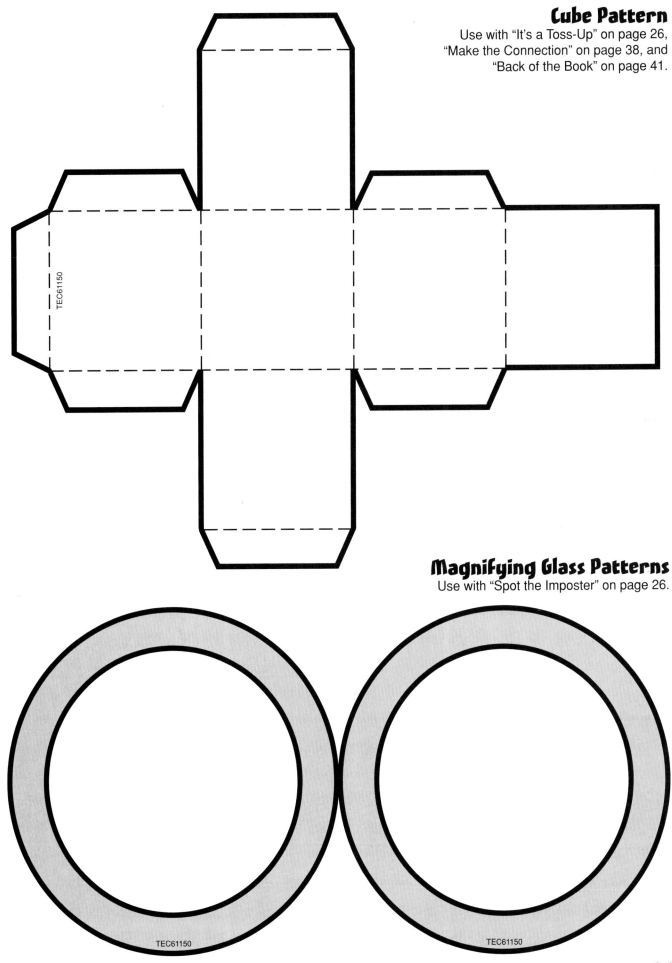

TEC61150

Magnifying Glass Patterns

Use with "Spot the Imposter" on page 26.

TEC61150

TEC61150

1 The mouse ran up the clock. Why did the mouse run up the clock? TEC61150	**2** The clock struck one. Do you think it is 1:00 AM or PM? TEC61150	**3** The mouse ran down. Where was the mouse going? TEC61150
1 Jack and Jill went up the hill to fetch a pail of water. Where on the hill would they find water? TEC61150	**2** Jack fell down. What caused Jack to fall down? TEC61150	**3** Jill came tumbling after. Why did Jill tumble after Jack? TEC61150
1 Little Miss Muffet sat on a tuffet. What is a tuffet? TEC61150	**2** Along came a spider… From where did the spider come? TEC61150	**3** And frightened Miss Muffet away. Why is she frightened of the spider? TEC61150
1 Humpty Dumpty sat on a wall. How did he get on the wall? TEC61150	**2** Humpty Dumpty had a great fall. What might have caused him to fall? TEC61150	**3** All the king's men couldn't put Humpty together again. Why couldn't they put Humpty together? TEC61150
1 Hey, diddle, diddle, the cat and the fiddle, What is a cat doing with a fiddle? TEC61150	**2** The cow jumped over the moon. How can a cow jump over the moon? TEC61150	**3** The dish ran away with the spoon. To where are the dish and spoon running? TEC61150

ba TEC61150	ss TEC61150	le TEC61150
ra TEC61150	ff TEC61150	er TEC61150
ta TEC61150	tt TEC61150	y TEC61150

Sentence Cards
Use with "Robust Writing" on page 31.

1. Today the class will play soccer. It will play on the soccer field.

   ___ ___ ___ ___ ___ ___ ___ ___ ___ ___.
   TEC61150

2. The music teacher teaches us to sing. She teaches us a song.

   ___ ___ ___ ___ ___ ___ ___ ___.
   TEC61150

3. The boys and girls walk quietly. They walk in the halls.

   ___ ___ ___ ___ ___ ___ ___ ___.
   TEC61150

4. Our teacher reads a story. He reads to our class.

   ___ ___ ___ ___ ___ ___ ___.
   TEC61150

5. My friends and I play kickball. We play during recess.

   ___ ___ ___ ___ ___ ___ ___.
   TEC61150

6. The fire alarm rang. It rang loudly.

   ___ ___ ___ ___ ___.
   TEC61150

Picture Cards

Use with "Seen But Not Heard" on page 32.

wreath reath reeth	gnot knot not	rap wap wrap
gnife nife knife	come comb colm	nabor nayber neighbor
light lite liht	knite knight gnite	crums cruhms crumbs
whey weigh way	write rite ryte	thum thumb tumb
nock gnock knock	gneel kneel neel	climb clime clighm

TEC61150

Picture Cards
Use with "Notable Nouns" on page 32.

Headline List
Use with "Homonymous Headlines" on page 34.

Cold Season Starts Early
Family Seal Found After 100 Years
Police Officer Takes a Bite Out of Crime
Bank Teller Complains About Change
Baseball Player Steals Home
Golfer Drives Ball Over 250 Yards
Mother Finds Baby in the Nursery
Young Teen Becomes a Star
Local Artist Draws a Crowd
Strange Object Found in Brush

TEC61150

Name _____ Recording sheet

On the Lookout

Cause (What Do I See?)	Effect (What Might Happen?)
1.	
2.	
3.	

Super Simple Independent Practice: Language Arts • ©The Mailbox® Books • TEC61150

Note to the teacher: Use with "Related Actions" on page 34.

Name_____

Comparing Fictional and Nonfictional Elements

Title:_____

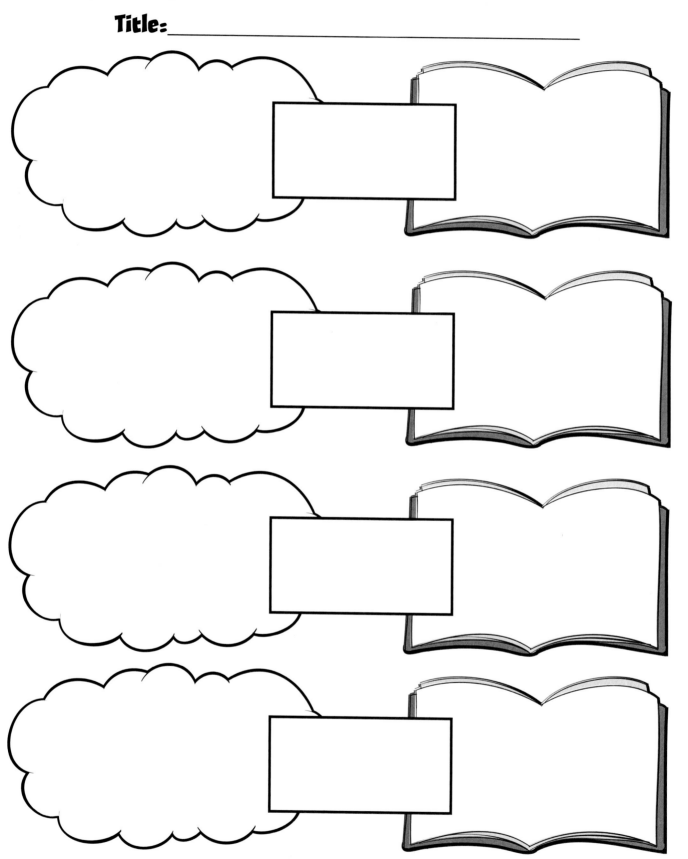

Note to the teacher: Use with "Could You Believe It?" on page 36.

Cell Phone Pattern

Use with "Communicating Ideas" on page 40.

Task Card

Use with "Sentence Builders" on page 41.

TEC61150

Tasks

1. Cut out three present-tense verbs. Use each verb in a different sentence.

2. Cut out two proper nouns and one verb. Use all three words in one sentence.

3. Cut out one present-tense verb. Use the present-tense verb in a sentence. Then rewrite the sentence in past tense.

TEC61150

Player 1 Score					Player 2 Score
		Connect 3			
een	ub	ap	aw	etch	eet
eam	atch	inkle	ead	out	ong
ape	unch	ut	ipe	ide	uggle
oll	ess	ike	ing	ain	ay

Super Simple Independent Practice: Language Arts • ©The Mailbox® Books • TEC61150

Note to the teacher: Use with "Make the Connection" on page 38.

The Great Prefix Race

Start	She <u>plays</u> the game <u>again</u>.	I <u>baked</u> the pie crust <u>ahead of time</u>.	Jill <u>folds</u> the towels <u>again</u>.	They took a math <u>test</u> <u>ahead of time</u>.
The batter was <u>mixed</u> <u>ahead of time</u>.	I <u>heated</u> my soup <u>again</u>.	Mom will <u>order</u> the cake <u>ahead of time</u>.	Dad <u>washed</u> the car <u>again</u>.	**Sneak Preview** Move ahead 2 spaces.

Directions for two players:
1. Place your game markers on Start.
2. Take turns flipping a coin and move as follows:
   - Heads = one space
   - Tails = two spaces
3. Name a word that uses a prefix to replace the underlined words in the box. If you cannot name a word, return the marker to the space where you began your turn.
4. The first player to reach Finish wins!

				Finish
The door had to be <u>locked</u> <u>again</u>.		He <u>read</u> parts of the book <u>ahead of time</u>.		The rabbit will <u>appear again</u>.
Review Time Move back 2 spaces.	Sam <u>paints</u> the walls <u>again</u>.		**Reflip the Coin**	
	She <u>cut</u> the string <u>ahead of time</u>.			

94

Super Simple Independent Practice: Language Arts • ©The Mailbox® Books • TEC61150

Note to the teacher: Use with "The Replace Race" on page 39.

Name _____

Story map

CHARACTERS

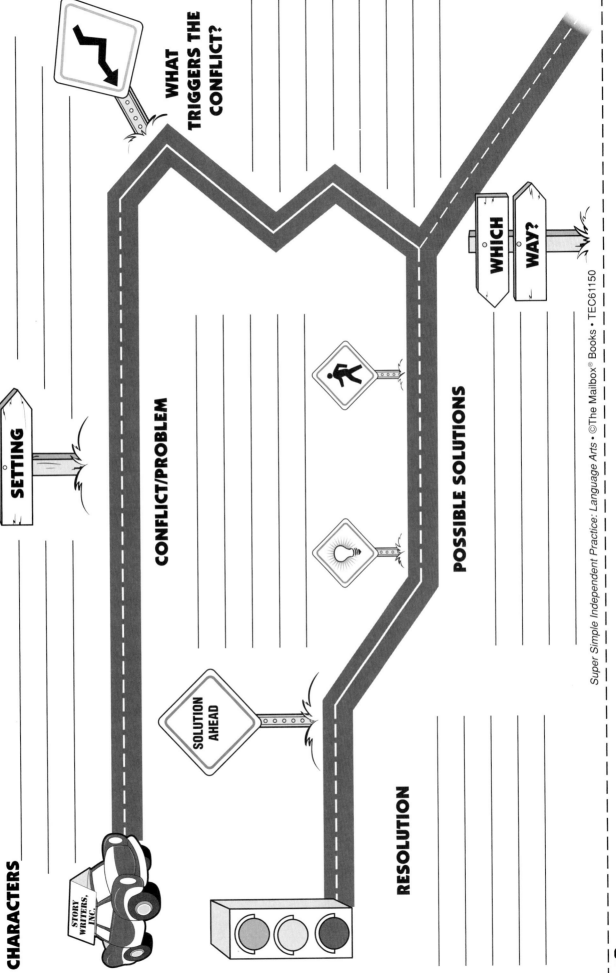

SETTING

CONFLICT/PROBLEM

WHAT TRIGGERS THE CONFLICT?

POSSIBLE SOLUTIONS

WHICH WAY?

SOLUTION AHEAD

RESOLUTION

STORY WRITERS, INC.

Super Simple Independent Practice: Language Arts • ©The Mailbox® Books • TEC61150

Note to the teacher: Use with "Sketch a Tale" on page 43.

Question Card

Use with "Roll and Respond" on page 46.

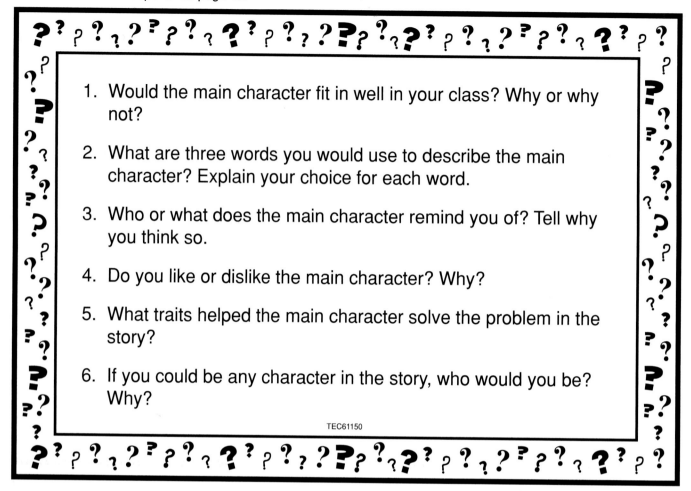

1. Would the main character fit in well in your class? Why or why not?

2. What are three words you would use to describe the main character? Explain your choice for each word.

3. Who or what does the main character remind you of? Tell why you think so.

4. Do you like or dislike the main character? Why?

5. What traits helped the main character solve the problem in the story?

6. If you could be any character in the story, who would you be? Why?

TEC61150

List of Facts

Use with "Handwritten Facts" on page 49.

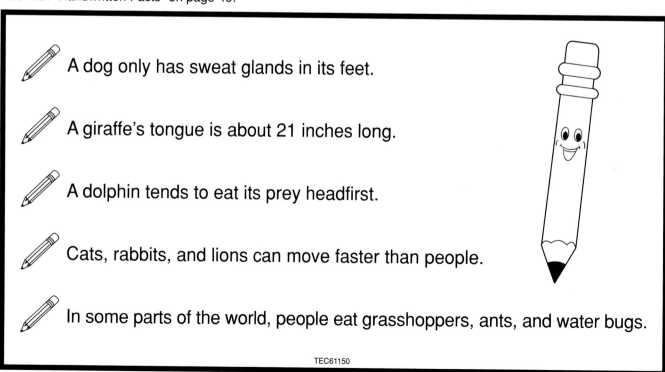

A dog only has sweat glands in its feet.

A giraffe's tongue is about 21 inches long.

A dolphin tends to eat its prey headfirst.

Cats, rabbits, and lions can move faster than people.

In some parts of the world, people eat grasshoppers, ants, and water bugs.

TEC61150

Use with "Now You're Talking!" on page 47.

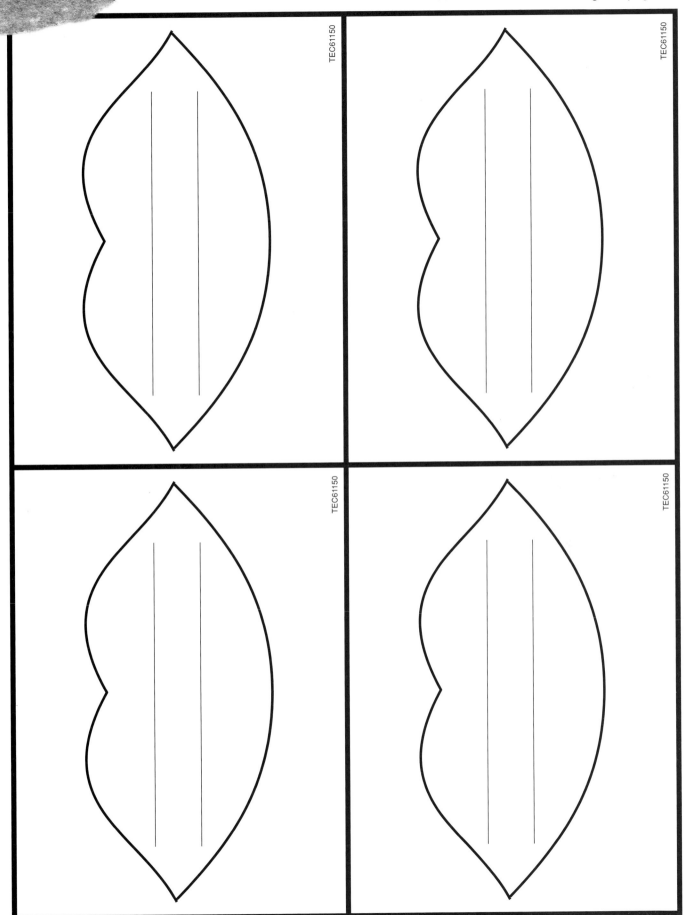

TEC61150

TEC61150

TEC61150

TEC61150

Possessive Noun Cards

Use with "Showing Ownership" on page 48.

farmer TEC61150	coach TEC61150	's	's
baker TEC61150	doctors TEC61150	's	's
boy TEC61150	men TEC61150	's	's
cats TEC61150	moms TEC61150	,	,
children TEC61150	partners TEC61150	,	,

Directions Cards

Use with "Making Choices" on page 48.

Direction Set A

How to Make a Spider

1. Use fabric glue to stick a large pom-pom to a small pom-pom.
2. Center the large pom-pom over four pipe cleaners.
3. Glue the pipe cleaners to the large pom-pom and let the glue dry.
4. Bend each pipe cleaner piece to make the spider's legs.
5. Glue wiggle eyes to the small pom-pom.

TEC61150

Direction Set B

How to Make a Spider

1. Glue two pom-poms together.
2. Glue on some pipe cleaners.
3. Bend the pipe cleaners.
4. Add eyes.

TEC61150

TEC61150

Name _____

Pause and Separate

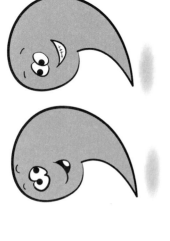

Complete each sentence.
Cut out the commas. Glue them where needed.
Copy each sentence on the line.

Write today's day and date.
Today is _____ _____ .

_____ .

Name your city and state.
I live in _____ _____ .

_____ .

Name three of your favorite foods.
My favorite foods are _____ _____ and _____ .

_____ .

What is something your teacher always says?
My teacher always says " _____ ."

_____ ."

Super Simple Independent Practice: Language Arts • ©The Mailbox® Books • TEC61150

Note to the teacher: Use with "Pause and Separate" on page 52.

, , , , , ,

1. "Did you hear about Goldilocks?" asked Hansel.

TEC61150

2. "No." What happened? asked Gretel.

TEC61150

3. "She went to the three Bears' house," said Hansel.

TEC61150

4. Gretel asked, "Did she eat their food again"?

TEC61150

5. Hansel said, "She ate some of Mama Bear and Papa Bear's food."

TEC61150

6. "Did she eat any of Baby Bear's food" asked Gretel?

TEC61150

7. "All of it said Hansel."

TEC61150

8. Gretel asked, "What happened? Were the bears mad?"

TEC61150

9. Hansel "replied, She was lucky this time. They were in a good mood."

TEC61150

10. "I wish she'd learn her lesson," said Gretel. "Do you want to see if she can come over?"

TEC61150

11. "Sure." Said Hansel. "Maybe we can all go for a hike in the woods!"

TEC61150

12. Gretel said, "I don't know about that, but I'll call her anyway."

TEC61150

Word, Phrase, and Apostrophe Cards

Use with "Extra Edits" on page 54.

a girls desk TEC61150	a dogs bone TEC61150
Im TEC61150	isnt TEC61150
ten birds nests TEC61150	my dads hat TEC61150
theyll TEC61150	shes TEC61150
weve TEC61150	two boys bats TEC61150

Name _____ Writing a poem

A.

_____
Rhyming Words

B.

_____
Rhyming Words

_____
topic

_____ A

_____ B

_____
rhyming word A

_____
rhyming word B

Note to the teacher: Use with "Rhyme Time" on page 55.

Poetry	Drama or Poetry?	Fiction or Poetry?
An example I know is	A couplet is an example.	There is a problem and a resolution.
Drama	Fiction or Nonfiction?	Drama or Poetry?
An example I know is	Third Grade Adventures on Mars might be an example.	A play is an example.
Fiction	Drama or Nonfiction?	Poetry or Nonfiction?
An example I know is	The dialogue is listed after the character's name.	Some of these rhyme.
Nonfiction	Fiction or Nonfiction?	Nonfiction or Poetry?
An example I know is	The Truth About Lions might be an example.	This might have realistic photos and captions.

TEC61150

Question Cards
Use with "Words to Investigate" on page 58.

1. What is the first entry in the index? TEC61150	2. What is the last entry in the index? TEC61150
3. What do the numbers in the entries mean? TEC61150	4. On what page(s) will you find information about _____? TEC61150
5. How is the index set up? TEC61150	6. Why do some words have extra entries underneath? TEC61150
7. What entry is listed after _____? TEC61150	8. What entry is listed before _____? TEC61150
9. How is an index helpful? TEC61150	10. How is an index like a glossary? How is it different? TEC61150

Grid Pattern and Cards

Use with "Covered Up" on page 60.

Word Bank		
Avenue	Captain	December	Doctor	feet	hour
inch	Junior	pound	Road	Street	Tuesday

		TEC61150

Dr.	Rd.	St.
TEC61150	TEC61150	TEC61150
Ave.	Jr.	lb.
TEC61150	TEC61150	TEC61150
ft.	Capt.	Dec.
TEC61150	TEC61150	TEC61150
Tues.	hr.	in.
TEC61150	TEC61150	TEC61150

Super Simple Independent Practice: Language Arts • ©The Mailbox® Books • TEC61150

Title: _____

Problem:

TEC61150

Title: _____

Problem:

Solution:

Solution:

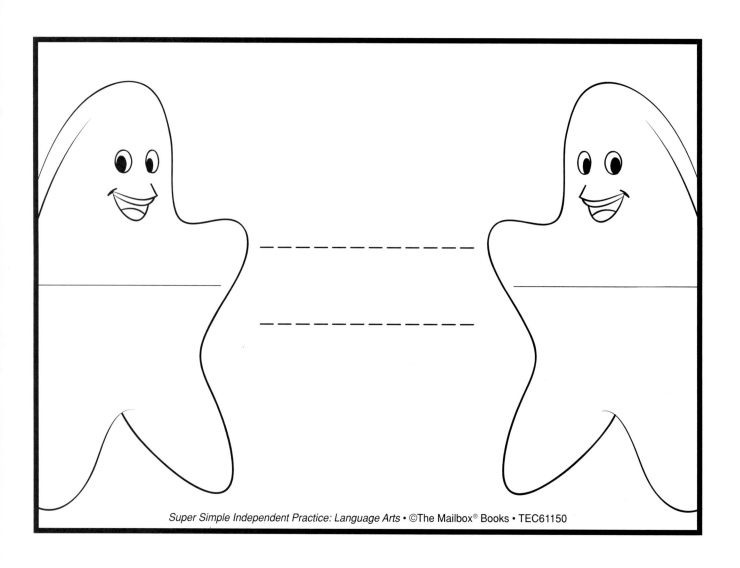

Super Simple Independent Practice: Language Arts • ©The Mailbox® Books • TEC61150

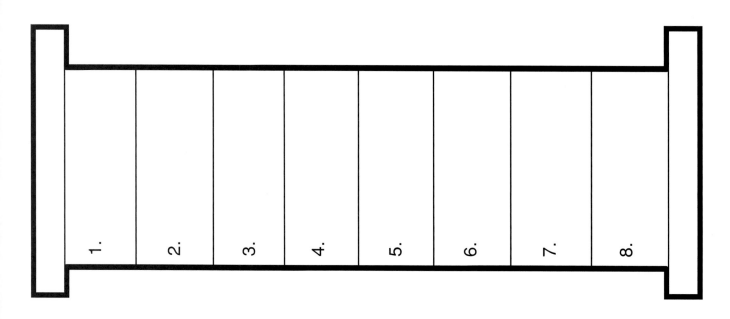

| 1. | 2. | 3. | 4. | 5. | 6. | 7. | 8. |

Note to the teacher: Use with "Fitting In" on page 62. Cut out the mat and strip and cut slits in the mat where indicated. Write a guide word on each line on the mat. Program the strip with words that would and would not be on a dictionary page between the named guide words. Thread the strip through the slits.

_____

_____

_____

_____

_____

_____

_____

_____

_____

_____

_____

_____

_____

_____

Note to the teacher: Use with "Published Pages" on page 63.

Idiom Cards

Use with "Figurative Phrases" on page 64.

to tell a secret	to get moving
let the cat out of the bag TEC61150	**shake a leg** TEC61150
to get married	have confidence
tie the knot TEC61150	**keep your chin up** TEC61150
a lot of money	everyone or everything
a pretty penny TEC61150	**across the board** TEC61150
a lot of fun	the person in charge (boss)
a barrel of laughs TEC61150	**the big cheese** TEC61150
very easy	leave to go somewhere
a piece of cake TEC61150	**hit the road** TEC61150

Dumbbell Pattern

Use with "In Training" on page 69.

Title ____________________

____

____

____

____

____

makes
me
think
about

____

____

____

____

____

____

TEC61150

Key Patterns

Use with "Keys to Pronunciation" on page 70.

Look for ____________________

Looks like ____________________

TEC61150

Look for ____________________

Looks like ____________________

TEC61150

Wheel A

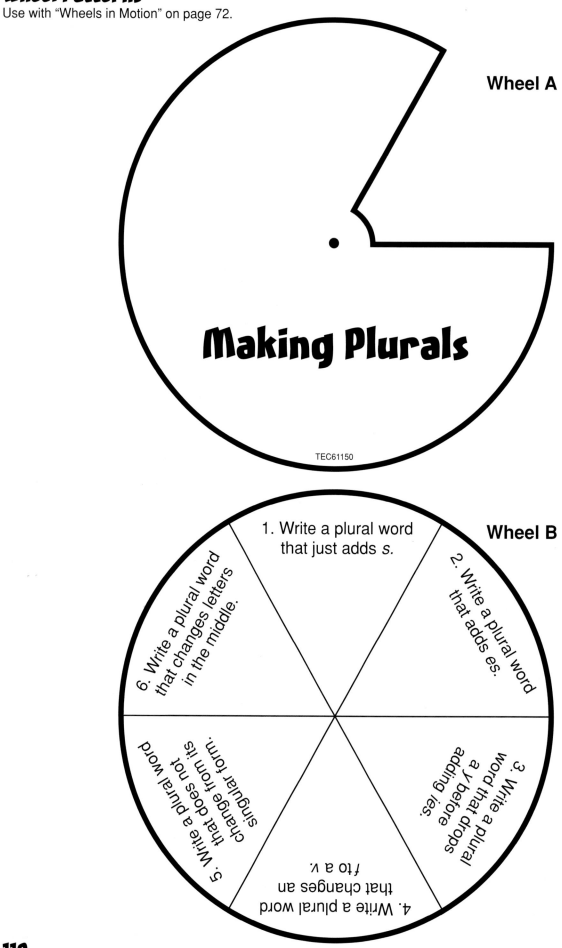

Making Plurals

TEC61150

Wheel B

1. Write a plural word that just adds *s*.

2. Write a plural word that adds es.

3. Write a plural word that drops a *y* before adding *ies*.

4. Write a plural word that changes an *f* to a *v*.

5. Write a plural word that does not change from its singular form.

6. Write a plural word that changes letters in the middle.

Skills Index